A
Change of
Habit

4-29-06 Shelley!
To dear contents of the
May the contents of the
this book of unify and grace
have mercy, and grace
of God: (Eph. 3:20, 21)
In Him! Joanie A. Howe

A
Change of
Habit
By Joanne Howe

Christian Communications
P.O. Box 150
Nashville, TN 37202

A CHANGE OF HABIT

Copyright © 1986 by Gospel Advocate Co.

Published by Christian Communications
A Division of Gospel Advocate Co.
P.O. Box 150, Nashville, TN 37202

ISBN 0-89225-292-8

Dedication

*T*his book is dedicated to my mother, whose joy and zest for life have been my strongest support in times of prosperity and persecution. Her steadfast love for God has been the foundation of my search for peace and happiness.

Contents

Foreword

*B*eing deeply involved in a research project and struggling against a deadline, the insistent ringing of the telephone was an unwanted interruption.

Little did I dream that the caller would involve me in a most challenging journey, a journey filled with pain—pain for the counselee as well as for the counselor. During this journey there would be a mixture of joy and laughter over a newly discovered truth. Many times we shared tears brought on by what the counselee called "the ripping and tearing."

Through the course of that journey I learned many things—and, I hope, imparted a small amount of knowledge.

In one session the words of Job, chapter 7, came to mind: "I will not refrain my mouth; I will speak in the anguish of my spirit; I will complain in the bitterness of my soul. Why hast thou set me as a mark against thee so that I am a burden to myself? When I say my bed shall comfort me, my couch shall ease my complaint; then, thou scarest me with dreams, and terrifiest me through visions."

Though the words were not used by the author, time and time again the essence of the message came through during the struggle.

During the process, extreme resistance to some truths would produce tears and anguish; but always present was the desire to be free from the haunting awareness that something, indeed, was wrong.

When from the cradle one has been so indoctrinated to a particular belief that finally he relinquishes all freedom of choice to embrace a lifestyle that is defined by the "authoritative" teaching of other human beings, he becomes a victim of mental and emotional enslavement that produces deep and abiding anguish. I have often wondered if this only happens to those who walk by blind faith. I am aware of the doubts that confront Christians in an alien world, but blind faith is another thing.

The human struggle is as old as mankind and as unique as the individual. For Joanne, this struggle was both unusual and painful; however, its outcome was victory in the glorious freedom of the Son of God's redeeming love.

This journey was a battle between the enslavement of the past and a hopeful future. You, the reader, take this journey with Joanne in A CHANGE OF HABIT.

March 1986
Lynn Paul Coffman

Acknowledgments

I am indebted to numerous Christians and Roman Catholics who contributed to this manuscript. In particular, I express my gratitude to Dr. Paul Coffman, who through his alertness and compassion for "lost souls" led me to the truth contained in God's Word; to Lydia Holby, whose love, loyalty, and friendship have been a joyful experience; to Dan and CeeCee Groghan, whose humility and commitment to God's Word have been a source of influence and encouragement; to Marion Barnette, my best friend and a positive force in my life; to Dennis Webber, whose dynamic energy spurred me on; to Diana Corley and Terry Herndon, who got me started; to Batsell Barrett Baxter, who encouraged me to stand firm for the truth; to Marianne Gscheidle, whose professional expertise initiated the editing of this manuscript; and to Virginia Garrison, with my deepest appreciation and admiration for her expert editing skills and spiritual insight.

I owe a special "thank you" to Don Humphrey, Vice-President of the Gospel Advocate Company, for his gentle patience and dedication to publishing this manuscript, and to Dan Van't Kerkhoff and Thomas Cook, who paved the way and opened doors so that my story could be told.

I thank the Holy Spirit for His guidance and wisdom as I applied pen to paper.

Preface

Since my delivery from the slavery of sin into a peaceful and happy life with God, I have felt a burden for those who are searching for the truth as taught in God's Word—especially Roman Catholics. Because of this feeling, I have chosen to share my heritage, training, beliefs, practices, and experiences as a Roman Catholic nun for nineteen years.

The birth pangs of this book were twofold: wrestling with the most Godly way of telling the truth in love, and maintaining a fierce commitment to beating Satan at his game of enslaving lost souls in ignorance and confusion. If one life is changed by this testimony, it will be eternally worth the tears, joys, and love that comprised these writing efforts.

All quotations are taken from the *New American Bible*, St. Anthony Guild Press, Patterson, N.J., 1970. Names and places are fictitious in some areas to avoid embarrassment or hurt to people and institutions.

Many teachings, training procedures, and traditions of convent life revealed in this book are, in most part, no longer practiced in American religious communities, with the exception of those religious who live a cloistered life. However, the underlying principles of submission to Church traditions and teachings are held as the spiritual directives for the member's walk with God.

After the Vatican Council in 1962, the Roman Catholic Church witnessed a tremendous exodus. People fled from confusing doctrines, inadequate theology, and perplexing questions to a state of religious indifference and apathy, or a hunger for the truth. Much of this discontent continues to this day. Many Roman Catholics have been led into counterfeit religious philosophies that so resemble the truth that it is impossible to distinguish between them and truth except by a *knowledge* of the Bible.

I invite the reader to journey with me as I search for directives and guidelines to purge my soul of ignorance, guilt, and sin. It is my prayer that you read this testimony with an open mind and questioning heart.

Again, let me emphasize that I have a deep, abiding love for my people. I cannot deny the rich, cultural heritage I thrived on for thirty-six years, but like the apostle Paul,

"I have come to rate all as loss in the light of the surpassing knowledge of my Lord Jesus Christ. For His sake I have forfeited everything; I have accounted all else rubbish, so that Christ may be my wealth and I may be in him, not having any justice of my own based on the observance of the law. The justice I possess is that which comes through faith in Christ. It has its origin in God and is based on faith. I wish only to know Christ and the power flowing from his resurrection; likewise to know how to share in his suffering by being formed into the pattern of his death. Thus do I hope that I may arrive at the resurrection of the dead!" (Philippians 4:8-11).

1
Reflections of Early Years

*T*he steeple bells pealed the message that my wedding ceremony was about to begin. With trembling hands, I picked up the daisy bouquet I was to carry up the aisle of the main chapel. I was nervous, frightened, and overwhelmed with excitement, but at the same time comfortable with the decision I had made.

Waiting for the organ to sound the processional hymn, my memory reflected on all that had caused me to make such a serious commitment: my twin sister's death, my mother's influence, my father's heritage, my brother's disappearance, my vow to God, my aunt's life in the convent, my grade school days, my entrance into the preparatory school, and my life as a postulant. Whether from fear, ignorance, confusion, innocence, or the glamour and sanctity portrayed of life in the convent, I concluded that God had a plan for my life, and He would reveal His desires to me as His Bride.

Little did I know that this ceremony would be but the beginning of an excruciating, soul-searching and God-seeking effort that would lead me to a greater understanding of His will and a Scriptural union with Jesus and His Bride for all eternity. What events led up to this revelation? Somberly, I reflected back to the days of my early childhood.

Early Childhood

Born on October 11, 1935, in Pittsburgh, Pennsylvania, I was the first of eleven children given by God to devout Roman Catholic parents. I shared the limelight with my twin sister, Jeanne, who was born several minutes after my presentation. I was a carbon copy of my mother with blonde hair, round face, distinct features, and bubbly personality. Jeanne resembled my dad with her dark brown hair, big brown eyes, oval face, and subdued disposition. As the firstborn, we were perfection-in-miniature to our parents.

Married during the post-depression period, my parents struggled to survive on my father's meager teacher's salary. Pinching pennies, they faced the economic pressures of a growing family, often doing their chores by the light of the sun or the streetlight that streamed into their two-room apartment.

I loved hearing stories about my baby days. My parents were unable to afford a bassinet for Jeanne and me, so we shared a wicker basket. How poor we must have been! Although I cannot recall those hardships, I know we were greatly loved and nurtured. One story of my life stands out more clearly than any other.

My mother told of feeding Jeanne and me our evening meal by the light from the streetlamp which shone brightly into our bedroom window. Suddenly, above our basket, a radiant light appeared. Startled, my mother looked up to see three nuns dressed in the habit of the Sisters of St. Joseph. They began speaking: "This one we will take home with us (pointing to my sister Jeanne), but this one (pointing to me), we will leave for awhile until her work is done." They departed as quickly as they had appeared. Frightened, my mother began praying to the Blessed Mother for courage and understanding of the strange event. Later, this supernatural experience would be recalled during a life-threatening situation.

The day before Thanksgiving, six weeks after our birth, Jeanne and I caught colds which gradually developed into pneumonia. Jeanne was extremely ill and was placed in a hospital. Since I was not as congested, mother cared for me at home.

The following morning, a policeman knocked on our door and told my father to go to the hospital immediately. Arriving there he found Jeanne in critical condition: she was not expected to live. Her big brown eyes opened wide, and she gave him a loving smile, as if to say goodbye before leaving for her Heavenly home. Within minutes, Jeanne curled her tiny hand around his fingers and, holding tightly, she breathed her last breath. Father never forgot that fateful day. In retrospect, I am convinced that mother's vision and mystical experiences affected my life and played an important role in my decision to become a nun!

Parents are like God to children. As the oldest, I was greatly influenced by my parents, especially my mother. Mom was the head and heart of the family. She taught us to pray and depend on God when we encountered the problems of life.

Growing up in the Russian Orthodox faith, mother developed a strong devotion to Mary, the Mother of Jesus. Often she told me stories about her own childhood experiences and of the ocean voyage from her native Russia to the United States.

Shortly before the Bolshevick Revolution in 1917, mother's family left their small village near Minsk and migrated to the United States. They hoped to find a new life, safe from the oppression that existed in their motherland, Russia. Life was difficult for her. Learning a new language and identifying with a strange new culture presented many challenges and fears. Although poor, she had plenty of warmth and love from two parents who believed in strong family ties and deep religious values.

As the oldest of five children (four born in America), mother established herself as an authority figure, and in her young adult life she provided sustenance for her family. When Christmas came, she made sure there were toys under the tree for her brothers and a turkey on the table. What a heritage she passed on to me, the oldest of her nine children!

Mother told of my grandfather's experiences as a Cossack. I pictured his fierceness and determination as a fighter. I was proud to be part Russian. Grandfather died when I was six years old, and this first experience of death was a time of great confusion.

I can still picture my grandfather in his coffin. What sadness I felt! Granddad was a real, life-like Santa Claus. I loved to sit on his lap and play with his moustache. I was sad and confused as people wined and dined around my grandfather's remains in his own living room, but since then I have come to understand and respect the customs of the Russian Orthodox faith following one's death. Family and friends rejoice rather than grieve. It is customary to drink and be merry, satisfied that the departed loved one is now happy in the land beyond this world.

Following his death, my mother recounted occasions when he appeared to her and warned her of impending disasters. My confidence in her was so great that I never doubted the reality of these encounters.

On her way home one evening after a long day shopping, mother took a familiar route through a densely wooded area near our home. As she walked along admiring the beauty and grandeur of nature, she was overwhelmed by a strange foreboding. Never before had she experienced this fear. Suddenly, a few yards ahead, her father appeared. Seeing him, she exclaimed, "Pop! What are you doing here?" There in the semi-darkness he cautioned her of danger ahead and instructed her to cross the street immediately. Without question, she ran the rest of the way home, never looking back. This was only one mystical experience that influenced my thinking.

Of German and Pennsylvania Dutch ancestry, my father grew up in an ethnic inner city neighborhood in Pittsburgh. He was seven when his father died of a heart attack. His widowed mother and two older sisters were his only role models in a religion that sees the man as the superior figure in authoritative positions—Roman Catholicism. At the age of 13 my father entered a preparatory school of the Divine Word Missionaries at Girard, Pennsylvania, a school which provided training for boys interested in the priesthood.

Three years after his entrance into preparatory school, his sister, Hazel, then 26, also entered religious life. Sister Edith (her name in religious life) lived to the age of 82, serving the Sisters of St. Francis for

57 years. Both my father and my aunt profoundly influenced my own future career and the choices I would make.

After 11 years of study and only three months before his ordination into the priesthood, my father met my mother. Overcome with her vivacity, fun-loving spirit, and intelligence, he fell in love and abandoned his life-long goal. They were quickly married in secret in the rectory of my father's childhood parish. In those days, a non-Catholic was not permitted to be married in a Catholic ceremony in the church building. Consequently, my parents sealed their vows to one another before God in the rectory, the living quarters of the local parish priest.

Before the marriage could be approved by the Roman Catholic Church, my mother was required to sign a document agreeing to rear in the Roman Catholic faith any children produced from the marriage. Not only did she conscientiously raise her children according to the dictates of Roman Catholicism, but she converted to its doctrines. As a commitment to her new faith, 11 children were conceived from the marriage.

My father was a gentle and loving man. Daily I waited on the front steps for his arrival home from work. He did most of the family shopping, and I loved to walk with him to the store, as if to "show off" the handsome father I owned. He only spanked me once, the day I sassed my mother. Sassing mother did not befit one who was an example to the younger children. The ultimate punishment was getting the "strap" from Dad! How humiliated and hurt I was! I could not imagine that my kind, loving father would spank his darling daughter! To keep the peace, he gave a few swats and sent me to bed without supper. Never again did I question mother's authority.

Discipline was only a small part of my childhood. Raised in a predominantly Roman Catholic, middle-class neighborhood, my home life was one in which strong religious values were stimulated and spiritual growth and intellectual pursuits encouraged. Because I was the oldest, I was rigidly trained in the rudiments of Roman Catholicism. Wishing to please my parents, I was strongly idealistic, taking care to adhere precisely to Catholic doctrine, and my mother's authority. Every aspect of my life was centered on pleasing Jesus. When I failed, I was cautioned that I was hurting Jesus and that I would go to Hell. I was taught to fear God and to love Him at the same time.

At a very early age I became aware of the solemnity of the Mass and the sacredness of Holy Communion. From my mother's instructions and the nuns' teachings, I knew that receiving the Sacrament of Holy Eucharist was truly a momentous occasion! I believed that Jesus was actually present: body, blood, soul, and divinity. I longed to receive Jesus into my heart at my first Holy Communion.

Receiving Holy Communion would lift me into the adult world of the

My first communion, age 7.

Catholic religion, where the Eucharist was the very core of Godly worship. Soon, I would have a relationship with Jesus that would be my greatest aid in leading a holy life as a Roman Catholic!

To establish this special relationship, I had to make my First Confession. I was told in catechism class that because of the sins of Adam and Eve I was unable to receive God's special graces. Only through the power of the priest in confession would all my sins be pardoned and a life of grace restored to my soul. Only then could I receive Holy Communion.

Eager to be a worthy candidate, I willingly and anxiously confessed every sin I could possibly remember in seven years of life. After saying a penance of three Hail Mary's and three Our Father's prescribed by the priest, I was a worthy candidate for receiving Jesus.

Anticipation mounted! I spent a restless night watching the clock. Finally, the long awaited moment arrived. The priest stood over me chanting in Latin: "Corpus Domini nostri Jesu Christi custodiat animom tuam in vitam aeternam. Amen." "The Body of our Lord Jesus Christ keep thy soul unto life everlasting. Amen." In my heart I was now one with Jesus! Because of this powerful commitment, I believed that if it was His will I would become His bride. This was the greatest gift I could give to God for all that he had done for me. I was convinced He would grant my wish.

Wearing a new, white, eyelet dress and carrying a small white prayer book and rosary beads I had been given, I marched down the aisle to be greeted by my parents in the church vestibule. They hugged me and told me how proud they were. Thrilled with joy, I went home to celebrate this wonderful day.

There I was greeted with a marvelous surprise! My aunt, Sister Edith, had taken a doll and dressed it in a nun's habit. I was delighted! Curiously, I examined its contents. How was it made? What was hidden under the black material? How were the white linens attached to the head? Did the nuns ever get hot wearing them? Did they take them off at night? How did they wash them? In years to come, I was to discover these hidden secrets and many more.

Family Crisis

Listening to the organ in the choir loft of the Motherhouse chapel, I pondered the events that led to the fulfillment of my childhood wish. I recalled the single event that led me to vow my life to God.

A tragedy during my tenth year of life still brings tears and heartaches. On July 15, 1946, my brothers, Raymond (nine) and Richard (six), and my sisters, Edith (five) and Geraldine (eight), headed for the Highland Park pool in Pittsburgh for an afternoon of swimming. Since I was in charge, Mom told me when she expected us home for supper. The hours passed swiftly as we romped and swam to our hearts' delight.

The oldest of 9 children, second from left.

Around 4:00, I began to gather the children for the journey back home. The walk would take at least an hour, and I wanted to be home on time. Raymond was nowhere in sight! Frantically, I searched the pool area and the nearby grounds. At last I spied him fishing in a small lake near the pool. I told him we would wait one-half hour at the end of the park. If he was not there at that time, we would return home without him. I cautioned him about the consequences should he not be home by suppertime. Raymond shrugged his shoulders and told me to go on home without him. After waiting the half hour, I went home without Raymond.

The evening wore on, Raymond had not returned. My mother sent us to bed early and said that she would handle Raymond when he came home.

At 11 o'clock that night, I heard unusual noises coming from the kitchen downstairs. Creeping down the steps, I could hear my mother crying and saying: "If he isn't home by now, he'll never return!" Neighbors gathered in our home to comfort her and reassure her. Distraught, I ran to her side crying, "Oh, Mommy, if only I had stayed and waited for Raymond, this wouldn't have happened!" She held me close and hugged me, assuring me it was not my fault.

Soon, my father came home from work. Daddy was a trainsman for the Pennsylvania Railroad, and he worked irregular hours. This particular night, he arrived home at 1 A.M. I will never forget his reaction when mother told him the news. Grief-stricken, he sat on the edge of their bed and cried softly "My son, where are you?" It was so unusual to see my father cry, and the echo of his plea still lingers in my memory. I was overwhelmed by his anguish. I loved him and wanted to take away the hurt.

For 40 dreary days and restless nights the family waited for clues concerning Raymond's whereabouts. A constant stream of reporters, detectives, and policemen worked diligently to locate Raymond. Initially, they suggested that he might be a runaway. My parents fiercely denied this allegation. He was a good boy, an altar boy, mischievous at times but obedient in important matters.

Fearing foul play, the *Sun-Telegraph News* and the *Pittsburgh Press* printed headline news of my brother's disappearance. Pictures showed a family saddened by the loss of one they loved and cherished. Rewards were offered for information about Raymond, dead or alive. One of the most massive searches in the history of Pittsburgh was initiated. In the Homewood-Brushton area of Pittsburgh where we lived, churches set aside Sunday, August 11, 1946, as a day of prayer, asking God to guide those involved in my brother's search.

My heart ached for my parents. Tormented, anxious, and sleepless, they waited patiently for some word or faint hope. One night, as I knelt to pray, I promised God that I would become a nun and dedicate my life to His service if He would reveal Raymond's location.

The next morning my prayers were answered. The head of the Missing Persons' Bureau broke the tragic news to my parents that Raymond's remains had been recovered from a densely wooded area several miles from our home. A year later we discovered that he had died defending himself against a 22-year-old sex deviate and molester of boys.

It was a very real, faith-building experience. God had heard me and had taken me at my word! I renewed my vow because He answered my prayer. When I cried out to Him, when I needed Him, He heard me!

Life became secure once again. My responsibilities increased as two more children joined the family. During my brother's disappearance, mother suffered a miscarriage. Shortly thereafter, another child was stillborn. Two years after Raymond's death, two darling little girls brought her joy and happiness, cushioning the grief and heartache.

Following my mother's footsteps, I established myself as a family figure. I was the natural example, both educationally and spiritually, for my younger brother and sisters.

Grade school years passed quickly. Eager to play the piano, I walked several miles weekly to take lessons from my aunt, Sister Edith. Waiting my turn outside the music room, I loved to watch the nuns perform their various activities. They looked like angels from heaven as they glided about so effortlessly with a certain glamour that was holy in its appeal! I looked forward to the day when I would become one of them!

My parents knew I desired to enter the convent. Mother felt it was a direct calling from God, and she encouraged me. My father prayed that one of his children would pursue the religious life he had abandoned. He felt that my desire was a blessing from God, an answer to his prayer! He was happy and willing to give God one of his children in his place—especially his oldest!

When I was in the seventh grade a club was organized in our parish for anyone interested in becoming a nun. Many of my friends considered it sissified, and since I wanted to be part of the "gang" I decided not to join. I went to parties, played "Spin the Bottle," and developed a crush on one of the eighth-grade boys.

I became a very popular pianist at parties and was an outstanding accompanist for the school's plays and assemblies. I even held the honored position as organist for the church's devotions, a placement which would contribute to my future acceptability and desirability as a nun. Life was exciting and fulfilling!

Outwardly, it appeared that I had lost my enthusiasm to become a nun, but the desire never left my consciousness. I always admired the nuns. Although some teachers had been real tyrants, their dedication, status, and holy glamour still appealed to me!

In the eighth grade I made a serious decision. The school I had attended for eight years discontinued its high school program. I needed to choose another high school. I weighed my choices! My father suggested that I apply to the girls' preparatory school of the community to which my aunt, Sister Edith, belonged. The prospect thrilled me! Could this be an answer to the vow made several years before?

The application to the Sisters of St. Francis Preparatory School required two recommendations from grade school teachers. Naturally, I chose my two favorites.

Sister Bertrand, my fifth grade teacher, had nominated me for a scholarship to the "Tam-O-Shanter" class in downtown Pittsburgh. This program encouraged budding young artists, one from each school, in the Pittsburgh area. Selection to attend the Tam-O-Shanter class meant a three-year scholarship, and I was chosen over many others. The many artistic skills I acquired there would be used in my teaching career.

My fourth grade teacher, Sister Edwin, was very pretty, and she knew me like a book! She was the only teacher who ever paddled me, for cheating during a spelling test. I admired Sister Edwin's openness and also the deep love and concern she had shown during my brother's disappearance. In many ways, she was the kind of nun I wanted to emulate.

Both Sister Bertrand and Sister Edwin were delighted to learn of my choice, and they gladly responded to the questionnaire.

After several weeks, I received word that I had been accepted as an aspirant to the Preparatory School of the Sisters of St. Francis of Millvale, Pennsylvania. I was overjoyed. Soon I received a supply list for the coming year. I read the list eagerly! Blankets, towels, bedlinens, and toiletries were required. During school hours, I was expected to wear a uniform: dark blue dress with starched white collar and cuffs, a hairnet, long woolen stockings, granny shoes, and a corset of heavy stays. I grimaced at the thought of wearing such an outfit.

Many of my eighth grade friends were planning to attend Catholic high schools nearby, and two were entering various preparatory schools for boys interested in becoming priests. As far as I knew, I was the only girl planning to pursue the religious life. Gradually, I revealed my choice to my closest friends. Many congratulated me. I felt honored to have such a high calling.

During the summer, several going-away parties were held. The many gifts helped minimize the costs of purchasing the long list of required items.

As days and weeks merged into months, I became acutely aware of the tremendous step. I was leaving home! One of my uncles tried to dissuade me from entering the preparatory school. He felt that I was too young, too pretty, and too fun-loving, at the age of 13 to waste my life behind convent walls! Exceptionally naive by worldly standards, I protested his recommendations. My mind was made up. I was going to be a nun, and that was all there was to it! God would take care of me, though I did have some misgivings about leaving home.

On September 3, 1949, I completed packing two large suitcases. I said good-bye to my little sisters and brother. I wasn't sad because I was fulfilling my dream and honoring my vow. In my parents' eyes, I was God's special gift to them. I had been called apart from the world to represent our family in the vineyard of the Lord. To a Catholic, a child called to follow a religious vocation is in special favor with the Lord. Since this was my first time away from home, the next three years would prove to be emotionally, psychologically, and socially frustrating.

2
Pursuit of Happiness

Mt. Alvernia, the Motherhouse of the Sisters of St. Francis, had been very familiar to me from early childhood. Located on the north side of Pittsburgh, Pennsylvania, amid rolling hills and winding roads, it possessed a storybook beauty. Over the years, my sisters and brothers had played under the sturdy oaks and maples when Mother and Daddy visited my aunt, Sister Edith.

A long iron fence enclosed the community's possessions and gave boundary to its land. I was ecstatic. I was awed by the towering steeples and the imposing building that provided solitude, peace, and spiritual growth for its residents. Soon I would identify with the inhabitants of such majestic surroundings.

We arrived at St. Clare Hall, my home for the next three years. Known as "the Aspirancy," this new three-story structure housed preparatory students. Situated several hundred feet from the main building of the Motherhouse, the Aspirancy bore a newness and special appeal for those who were leaving home for the first time and entering a new way of life.

I walked with Mother and Daddy to the front door. It was evident in their smiles and gestures that they were very proud of me. I thought of the tremendous sacrifices they had so willingly made. I remembered my six sisters and one brother. I could see them all: Geraldine (the third oldest and the one who would fill my role as Mom's helper), Edith, Rosie, Ramona, and Richard and Henrietta, who would follow my example and choose preparatory schools for their high school education. Though my feelings for them were tender, I was confident that God would reward my sacrifice and watch over the family.

Warmly greeted by the Directoress of the aspirants, we were led into a large drawing room where I met Sybil, one of the older preparatory students. Sybil was to serve as my "spiritual sister" for the first few weeks of orientation. Sybil seemed pleasant enough, as she escorted my parents and me to the room we would share for the next six months. After showing me which side of the room was mine and telling my parents where to place my belongings, Sybil continued the tour. The Aspirancy was comprised of four classrooms, four large lavatories, a large recreation room, a small chapel, four small rooms for various individual activities, a music room, a kitchen, two offices, a large drawing room, and a huge laundry room, all attractive though simply decorated.

Joanne as a junior prep student.

The decor was indicative of the disciplined but happy, childlike life of the occupants. How jubilant I was to be one of them.

Soon it was time for my parents' departure. I felt a pang of loneliness as they held me close and assured me they would write soon and send some "goodies" as well. I overheard them tell the Directoress how privileged they felt to have their daughter in such a wholesome, refined environment.

Knowing that I would only see my parents on visiting Sundays once a month, I retreated with mixed feelings to the drawing room where we all met to walk to dinner in the main building of the Motherhouse.

Later, I met other girls who had all chosen the aspirancy as a new way of life. I looked forward to knowing them and making new friends.

Sleep came quickly that night, and thoughts of home and family were promptly laid to rest after a long day of excitement.

Early the next morning, I was awakened by the loud clamoring of a bell. Thinking it was the fire alarm, I hastily gathered valuables and hurried down the hallway seeking the nearest escape route. To my surprise, others were scurrying to and from the central lavatory, obviously unconcerned by impending disaster. Much to my relief and with a bit of embarrassment, I found that the bell merely served to usher in a new day. Laughing at myself, I returned to my room. Noting that I had 20 minutes before presenting myself in chapel, my roommate urged me to make the most of the time. I soon realized that strict observance of time was a priority.

After a short devotional in the small room called the oratory, I and my fellow aspirants were taken to the chapel in the main building of the Motherhouse. This chapel would be used for the majority of our religious functions.

After attending daily Mass, we proceeded to a small room known as the refectory. This was the aspirants' dining room, adjacent to the main dining room where the postulants, novices, and professed religious were served their meals. Having come from a large family, I was accustomed to "waiting my turn" and "family style" service from large dishes. I was not accustomed, however, to eating in total silence, and I felt very uncomfortable in such an atmosphere. Later that morning I learned the underlying principles behind such regimentation, as well as many other disciplines expected in my formative years.

Returning to St. Clare Hall, the 31 new freshies gathered in the large drawing room for a lecture on the advantages of preparatory life. Living in a religious atmosphere and under special direction during our developmental years would preserve, protect and foster the privileged vocation we were called to fulfill. Apart from the world's distractions, we would have time to think about our vocation and listen to the voice of God. With the assurance that every opportunity and help would be given to prepare us for the chosen life, the Directoress explained the "whys" of silence and self-denial as well as the rules governing our conduct with those in the main building across the road. We were to have *no communication* with the postulants and novices and very little communication with the professed nuns. If we chose to follow this rigorous training, we would lead healthy, happy lives with good mental, moral, and spiritual character. I wondered whether I would be equal to the sacrifices: rigorous schedules, academic programs, stern etiquette standards, archaic dress codes, limited recreation, disciplined behavior, and restricted communication both within and without the Aspirancy. Little did I know that these precepts would become my whole way of life in my adult years.

Goals dominated my thinking, and I willingly adjusted to the requirements of the preparatory school. Painful though it was, I willingly submitted to wearing a cumbersome uniform of dark blue serge with heavily starched white collar and cuffs, long woolen stockings, and granny shoes. My long blonde hair was pulled tightly in a hairnet behind my ears. Never did I question any rule or restriction. I was grateful for the opportunities.

My day began at 6:00 A.M. with morning prayers, daily Mass in the main chapel of the Motherhouse, and breakfast. Classes began at 8:30. Each aspirant was assigned daily chores, such as dusting, mopping, or cleaning the lavatories on one of the three floors of the Aspirancy. These tasks were performed prior to our attendance at class. I remember the full-length apron I was required to wear over my uniform to prevent it from getting dirty.

My first assignment was cleaning the lavatory. I tried very hard to make the best of what I considered a demeaning task, and eventually I won the praise and admiration of the Directoress for being an "outstanding worker." I longed for the day when I would be assigned a more "refined chore" such as cleaning and dusting the oratory.

After daily classes, I returned to St. Clare Hall, where I changed from my uniform into a housedress for an evening of study and recreation. An aspirant's educational environment was built around a strong academic program preparatory to college entrance examinations. Homework was done in separate classrooms designated for freshies, sophomores, juniors, and seniors, respectively. Monitors, chosen by the Directoress, took the roll and presided over the study halls. They became known as "snitches" because of their tattling to the Directoress. On weekdays, study time lasted for an hour after school and resumed for two hours after dinner. No one was ever permitted to do homework in the privacy of her bedroom. Everything was done in a group setting.

Grades were carefully scrutinized. Anyone receiving a grade below "C" was reprimanded and given penances, such as restriction from after school activities or from special weekend functions such as wiener roasts and picnic outings. The most painful penance involved the candy box. Each aspirant received a candy box at entry day, and it was customarily replenished monthly. A low grade meant an empty candy box. Fortunately, I did not experience these punishments; however, several of my classmates were not so blessed! Pressure to produce, as well as stress and anxiety resulting from inability to perform, caused many classmates to forsake their vocations and return to the world. I felt sorry for them, yet I knew the rigorous programs were designed to test our ability to persevere. Eager to succeed, I was unaware of the further "acts of humility" with which I would be tested.

As a boarding student, I participated in a high school program es-

Her first visiting day while a student. (Picture taken in the graveyard of the Sisters of St. Francis.)

pecially for those in the Aspirancy. Mt. Alvernia was considered an exclusive girls' high school, and selected students from wealthy families were bussed there from areas around the city. These "day students" were assigned to classes with the preparatory students.

I can well remember watching those girls and wishing that I also had the freedom to come and go, to do what they did, to wear what they wore, or to experience what they talked about.

As I watched them board buses and return home, I felt a longing to be with my own sisters and brother, a longing to love and be loved. I wished that I could go to my own mother when I was perplexed and confused. Instead, I reminded myself that I was "special," and had committed my life to God. When troubled, I sought only the advice of my peers. The Directoress, I reasoned, would think me too weak to cope with the problems of life and growing up. Ultimately, I feared being sent home. Determined to succeed, I found various ways of escaping the normal adolescent problems. In later years I discovered this pattern pervading my whole life.

Going to classes, coming home, and changing clothes, followed by a half hour of outdoor physical exercise, three hours of study, and a half hour of indoor recreation became automatic behavior in my life. I welcomed the evening bell summoning everyone for devotions. The days were long and full, and I looked forward to a night's rest.

Evening devotions consisted of structured prayers said with arms outstretched for a period of five minutes, after which I retired to my room in total silence. The next hour was allotted for personal needs and preparation for the next day. Lights were turned off at 10:00 P.M. Anyone found in the hallways or bathroom after that time was reprimanded severely by the Directoress or her assistant. Rules were strict, and infractions against even the smallest ones were punishable by reprimands before the entire group of aspirants. Being accustomed to strong discipline at home, I resolved to obey every rule. How I feared public humiliation!

One Sunday morning, a month after my entrance into the Aspirancy, the Directoress rang the buzzer in her office, signaling the entire group to assemble in the large drawing room. Monthly, we gathered in this same room for a meeting of the "Tru-Blu" Club. This club furnished opportunities for self-expression and entertainment. Today, however, we assembled for more important matters.

With a look of stoicism, the Directoress reminded us how privileged we were to belong to the Aspirancy. Cautioning that with privileges also came responsibilities, she produced a basket of clothing from beneath her desk. Holding up several pairs of underpants, she voiced her disgust and disapproval of individuals who would throw soiled underpants down the laundry chute for someone else to launder. Was I guilty? Within seconds, I and three other students were called to the front of the room to claim our soiled clothing. Humiliated, I was rebuked severely for my actions and put on penance for the entire week. Crushed and sobbing, I returned to my seat, wishing I could disintegrate right on the spot! Why had I put my name on all my clothing? Later that day, the Directoress called me into her private office and explained her actions.

Joanne (right) with her mother on the monthly visiting day.

I never forgot that humiliating experience, and I carried a deep dislike for the Directoress from that day forward.

I missed home and family terribly during the three years in preparatory school. I can still remember the excitement as visiting Sunday arrived. I bubbled with enthusiasm at the sight of my mother and father. For several hours I'd spend some precious time with my younger sisters and brother. Disappointed when their visits ended, I yearned to go home with them. It was difficult not to cry. Yet I was proud to be an aspirant. I wanted to remain at any cost! Leaving family was part of the sacrifice of my calling.

My letters home were filled with plans for family activities at Thanksgiving, Christmas, Easter, and summer vacation. Outgoing and incoming mail was censored routinely. That, however, did not deter me from writing what I chose to write. In one letter my father pointed out misspelled or misused words. Henceforth, I used that letter as my private dictionary when writing home.

Extracurricular activities provided an excellent means of escape. With a background in piano, I learned to play the marimba. I also enrolled in the Saturday morning oil painting classes taught by a lay benefactor of the community. Between the marimba, oil painting, and participating in plays and operettas, I had little time for social recreation, except on weekends.

I continued to be initiated in the ways and means of religious discipline. Bed making, table setting, cleaning, washing, mending, darning, hairgrooming, and body cleanliness were tasks in which I became thoroughly efficient after the first year.

Saturday mornings were set aside for general cleaning and household chores; afternoons were for personal responsibilities. It was then that I washed and set my hair. I spent the rest of the time playing the piano or taking walks with some of the girls.

Colleen, as Irish as her name, proved to be a loyal friend and companion for three years. Since she was a pianist and artist as well, we shared common interests. During summer vacations we visited each other's homes and learned the art of give and take in a close relationship. In later years Colleen would leave the preparatory school for life as a cloistered nun in a Carmelite Monastery near her home in Johnstown, Pennsylvania.

Although I could spend summers at home, I was encouraged to attend daily Mass to help nourish my spiritual life and prevent distraction over worldliness. Dating and wearing makeup were forbidden at any time. Returning to the outside world after a year in the Aspirancy proved to be traumatic. Accustomed to strict supervision and austere living, I found worldly standards uncomfortable and incongruent with my principles of living.

By the junior year of high school, I was settled into the disciplines of religious life. I was proud that I had accomplished and survived two years of rigorous training. I was beginning to see progress toward the accomplishment of my goal.

During my senior year, I faced two choices: go home for the summer and join the Order of the Sisters of St. Francis in September, or join the Order in January of my senior year and make up unfinished subjects during college. Uncertain, I sought the advice of my parents.

Father felt that my experience in the outside world was too limited to enable me to make such a serious decision about the future. Reluctantly, and at his request, I entered another all-girl Catholic high school, closer to home. There I completed my senior year of high school.

3
The Postulancy

L ife at Sacred Heart High provided a sharp contrast to the tense, highly structured academic life at the Preparatory School. The friendly, relaxed environment and an atmosphere of warmth and acceptance enabled me to reestablish my identity with the outside world.

I was quickly accepted by students and faculty alike. Within weeks, I established new relationships and was invited to join several service clubs.

New, more positive feelings surfaced, and I began to enjoy my present life, though I still felt a strong pull to the past.

Memories of Mt. Alvernia

In this new environment I recalled the uncertainty and anxiety of the last day at Mt. Alvernia. I remembered clearly the confusion as I viewed former routines, close relationships, accustomed roles and familiar surroundings in one single concept—abandonment. Though many aspects of my role had been emotionally, psychologically, and physically constricting, I had derived a great deal of unconscious comfort and security in familiar routines and my identity as an aspirant.

While most of my classmates were eagerly awaiting summer vacation and planning their return to the Aspirancy in September, I would be leaving for good. I was confused and miserable. Unable to contain my frustrations, I sought the comfort of my best friend, Colleen.

One evening after a day of cleaning and packing, I asked Colleen to meet me on the north stairs of the third floor landing in St. Clare Hall. Often we had rendezvoused there to discuss problems and plan future events. Promptly at 10:00 P.M., the buzzer rang for "lights-out." I lay on my bed, waiting for the coast to clear. Stealthily, I opened the door, peered out, and crept down the long, dark hallway toward the north end of the building. I glanced back to see if I was followed. Finally, I found Colleen sitting on the top step of the stairways, anxious to talk.

I shared with her the decision that had been made regarding my senior year of high school. Unable to control myself, I wept softly. Consolingly, she put her arms around me and told me that she was also feeling anxious, but for a different reason. Softly and deliberately, she confided that she had recently been accepted by a cloistered community. She would be entering their Novitiate the following September. Her parents were reluctant to give their approval, for once they did, they would never again see or touch their daughter. Colleen's life as a discalced (barefoot) Carmelite Nun would be one of complete silence and harsh living. Once she took her vows, she would live behind the high walls of the cloister until her death. Only in rare instances did the Office for Religious Orders in Rome give their approval for the dispensation of the vows of discalced cloistered religious.

I listened in shock and disbelief. I was stunned! I had seen the high stone walls and barred windows, and I knew of the rigorous life behind cloistered walls. Colleen would be sleeping on a straw-filled pallet, eating dry bread and never eating meat, speaking only 15 minutes out of an entire day. I just couldn't believe that my best friend, Colleen, would submit to this kind of treatment. As dedicated as I was in following Jesus and becoming His Bride, the thought of remaining in a cloister, shut away from human experiences, love, and life itself until death was unbearable. Forgetting my own dilemma, I begged her to reconsider. I reassured her that I was her friend, and I would support her in whatever way I could. We talked for several more hours, making plans to visit each other during the summer months. As upset as I was over abandoning my own vocation at the preparatory school, I was more concerned about Colleen. In the wee hours of the morning, I returned to my room, burdened by her revelation.

In the early morning of June 2, 1952, my father came to take me home for a permanent stay. I felt a surge of nostalgia for the past three years at Mt. Alvernia. Mustering up courage to say goodbye, I gave a round of hugs to all who came to say farewell for another year. Colleen had left very early that morning for Johnstown, Pennsylvania. Though separated, we had sworn our faithfulness to each other the night before, vowing to forever remain close friends. Unfortunately because of distance and complexity of events, this commitment would never be fully honored.

As the car rounded the driveway, I looked back to see the buildings of the Motherhouse clustered at the top of the hill. Soon, the towering domes and imposing structures were hidden by green summer foliage. I determined to make the best of the new circumstances and challenges in store for a sixteen-year-old.

A loud, clanging bell returned my thoughts to Sacred Heart High and my new surroundings. I was feeling a renewed buoyancy and excitement as future plans evolved. I was drawing for the school newspaper, assisting in several service clubs, going to parties, making new friends, and learning my way around town on a streetcar. I was adapting and excited about the opportunities that lay ahead! I took pride in my ability to handle the challenges of secular life. I looked forward to sharing my adventures with friends from the preparatory school who would soon be entering the Postulancy.

High school graduation, June, 1953.

Christmas was special for those entering the Postulancy in January. During this festive season, family and friends gathered, not only to exchange gifts but to extend their blessings and approval to aspirants entering religious life. The Roman Catholic Church had always held those in the clergy and religious life in the highest regard, and they were extremely proud of those who dedicated their lives to God as their official representatives before Him. Consequently each candidate would be showered with money, praise, and adulation. Since this would be the last visit home, many families celebrated her departure at this special time. I received several invitations to attend these events.

Since leaving Mt. Alvernia in June, I had not communicated with anyone who had returned to the Preparatory School the following September. A policy existed which forbade those remaining in the Aspirancy to have any correspondence with those who left for the outside world. Knowing of the strict enforcement of this rule, I declined the invitations I received, claiming an extraordinary amount of school work and family responsibilities. The truth was that I felt like an intruder and an outsider now. I expressed my happiness for them via letters and assured them I would join them the following September. As committed as I was to this intention, I could not foresee the future God had in store for me.

Adapting to family life was an adjustment. The tranquil life at school had created a tunnel vision of family life. *Real life* meant noise, confusion, and the constant activities of seven growing children. *Normal family life* meant helping the younger ones with school work, household chores, cleaning, ironing baskets and baskets of clothing, shopping and settling disputes. Having been severed from my family for three years, I needed a lot of love, support, and understanding.

Class assignments were relegated to late at night when everyone was asleep, and I could focus on the material needed to maintain my educational performance. During this time, Mother and I would often share the day's achievements and frustrations, renewing the strong bond we had enjoyed over the years. I expressed my guilt feelings and anxieties. Her continued love and support helped heal the emotional scars of the past three years. Sensitive to my restlessness and nostalgia about convent life, she encouraged me to pursue my dream. Opportunity to realize this goal came shortly after the Christmas holidays.

Two of my former grade school classmates were planning to attend a weekend retreat at the Motherhouse of the Sisters of St. Joseph in Baden, Pennsylvania. Aware of my strong religious convictions, they invited me to the retreat. Delighted by the opportunity to be in an environment of prayer, meditation, and soul-searching, I accepted their invitation. This decision was to change the course of my life for the next 16 years.

The drive to Baden took almost two hours. During the journey, my friends, Nora and Mary Anne, chattered aimlessly, reminiscing occasionally about teachers, humorous events, and classmates.

A light, cool April breeze rustled the air. Its freshness soothed our faces as we delighted in the marvelous country smells of herbs, bark, and rich soil. How peaceful it seemed! Completely surrounded by old oaks with low extended boughs, the Motherhouse in Baden seemed genuinely appealing to all who entered its portals.

At the main entrance we were greeted graciously by two smiling postulants. They directed us to the area where we were to spend the weekend learning about the service of the community to others and their principles of commitment to God.

During the next two days, the desire to commit my own life to God became overwhelming. Never before had I sensed God's nearness and deep love as I did now. Never before had I so fervently prayed. Never before had I experienced His presence as I did at this retreat. With renewed strength and courage, I resolved to enter the community that was instrumental in my early formation—the Sisters of St. Joseph from Baden, Pennsylvania. They had always been my first love, and I wanted nothing more than to identify with a group of dedicated nuns who had shown me such great love and affection. I was convinced that God's hand was guiding me. I was anxious to return home and share this wonderful news with my parents.

On Sunday morning, the last day of the retreat, we were given the privilege of attending Mass with the entire community present in the main chapel of the Motherhouse. Seeing hundreds of nuns, postulants, and novices worshipping God in unity, my heart was stirred to an even higher level of love. I sensed God's Presence in that august body. The desire to become one with them became my paramount goal from that day forward.

On the way home, I thought about the weekend events. Everything had happened so quickly. Surely, the Hand of God had been directing me toward this community.

Since I had been raised in a deeply religious atmosphere, faith in God was a very real part of my life. Believing in God's providence, mother had stressed that if we acknowledge Him in our lives, He will direct our paths. Although she never told me, she had been convinced since my twin sister's death that my future would be as a Sister of St. Joseph.

Over the next few months, a chain of events prepared me emotionally, physically, and spiritually for the most important step in my young adult life.

I regularly corresponded with several of the postulants from the weekend retreat. Terry, one of the oldest, took a special interest in me because of my younger sister's friendship with her younger sister, Susan.

She and the other postulants wrote letters, vibrating with the excitement and happiness of convent life. More than anything else, I wanted to become part of a group that exuded beauty and radiance from within. They all encouraged me to submit my application to the Mother Superior (who at that time was Mother Mary Grace) for admission into their community. Overwhelmed by the attention and encouragement, I made my decision to enter the Sisters of St. Joseph the following September.

After school one day in early May, I received a letter postmarked "Sisters of St. Joseph, Baden, Pennsylvania." Unable to contain my excitement, I threw my books on the front porch, tore open the letter, and eagerly read its contents. They acknowledged my desire to enter their community. A physical examination had been arranged for me at the community's hospital on the north side of Pittsburgh. Included in the letter was a questionnaire to answer and return to the Motherhouse as soon as possible. At the end were words of advice from Mother Mary Grace. She encouraged involvement in heartfelt prayer and devotion to Mary the Mother of Jesus who dedicated her life in doing God's will. As Mary's life consisted of the single honor of intimately helping Christ accomplish His work of salvation, so my life would be a call to double for Mary in Christ's Church. I felt very humble and extremely honored! I had not only received a personal letter from the Mother Superior of over 700 religious, but she had asked me to help fulfill the role of God's Mother in the Roman Catholic Church. Such a responsibility was awesome.

That evening, my parents helped me with the lengthy questionnaire. Some questions were puzzling: "Had I a certificate of Baptism and Confirmation? Had my parents a good reputation in the community and had they lived virtuous and edifying lives? Had my parents ever been under repute for any enormous crime? Did I enjoy good health and have the strength necessary for the discharge of the duties of the community? Did I have good sense and judgment and was I capable of understanding the spiritual and temporal things necessary for my salvation and the discharge of the employments of the community? Had I ever given great scandal in my life? Had there ever been any insanity within my family background? Was I predisposed to hysteria? Would I be liable or would the community be liable for a lawsuit of any kind because of some crime on my part? Had I maintained my virginal purity? Was I entering the community under any kind of coercement, or was I entering of my own free will?" Not only did I sign the questionnaire, but it was also signed and sealed by a Notary Public. My father explained the document's legal ramifications and its impending results should I have falsified my statements. I was confident that I had responded with honesty and integrity.

Several weeks after returning the questionnaire to the Motherhouse, after completing a thorough physical and psychological examination and forwarding my academic transcripts, I received a letter of acceptance. I eagerly anticipated the day when I would end life in a secular world and begin training as one of God's chosen—a nun. I was anxious to share my joy with friends and relatives.

My parents were delighted. They felt very honored that their daughter had been chosen to represent the family in the vineyard of the Lord. My aunt, Sister Edith, was disappointed that I was not entering her community. She felt cheated of the joy of having one of her own nieces in the same community.

I received letters of congratulations from several friends in the Postulancy at Mt. Alvernia. Although they were saddened at my decision to enter the Sisters of St. Joseph rather than the Sisters of St. Francis, they were unanimous in their wholehearted support.

In March of my senior year, I had been recruited as an operator by Bell Telephone Company. Undecided at that time about my future, I had accepted a trainee position in the East Liberty Office in Pittsburgh, Pennsylvania, several blocks from high school. By June, I was working the switchboard and enjoying the challenges of serving the public. The training supervisor was very sweet, patient, and understanding of the naivete of a young high school student. I learned quickly under her tutelage and admired her greatly. When I told her of my decision to enter the convent, she wished me happiness, but with regrets. Unknown to me at that time, I was to have been transferred to the business office the following week as a promotion because of my excellent performance as an operator. I was assured by the chief operator that should I ever leave the convent I would be rehired immediately. I was pleased with this acknowledgment from my immediate supervisor.

I felt even more like a celebrity as friends and family cheered me on toward the goal. Mother would tease me and tell me I had more friends than "Heinz had varieties." Farewell parties, gifts, and words of praise brightened every corner of my life. Entrance day into the convent drew near.

At 10:00 A.M. on September 8, 1953, the telephone rang loudly. Mother was dressing my two youngest sisters, Rosie and Ramona, for the long journey to the Motherhouse in Baden. Daddy was in the bathroom shaving, and I was packing the last of the items for my new life in the convent. The rest of the children had been sent to school. There were too many for a car that seated only six people. Rushing upstairs, I picked up the telephone and heard a voice say: "Is this the Howe residence?" "Yes," I replied. The voice on the other end then said: "This is St. Francis Hospital calling. We are sorry to inform you that Mrs. Mary Howe died 15 minutes ago." Shocked and stunned, I thanked the caller and quickly hung up. Almost simultaneously, Daddy opened the bathroom door and asked who called. Sitting on the hallway floor, confused and bewildered, I tearfully blurted out, "Oh, Daddy, what are we going to do? Grandma just died!" As if only yesterday, I can still see my father's tears. "We're going to Baden, darling", he said, "and nothing will interfere with your mission in life, not even my mother's death!" I knew what Daddy had said was true. My father would never allow anything to interfere with duty. I knew also that Grandma would have wanted it this way. Only the day before, I had visited her. Whispering through the oxygen tent, she had told me how proud she was of me and cautioned me to allow nothing to interfere with my decision to become a nun. Her last words were "Persevere to the end, Joanne!" As distraught as I was over Grandma's death, I felt strengthened by her parting words of advice. My grandmother's death and the completion of my trip to Baden that tragedy-filled day underscored the fact that nothing—absolutely nothing—would interfere with my commitment to God and His service.

As the door closed behind me and the last piece of luggage was loaded, a numbness came over me that I would remember years later. Looking at my little sisters, two and three years old, I realized I would miss most of their maturity. I would be unable to help them through the struggles of puberty and adolescence. I had missed all the group support, encouragement, and involvement during my adolescent years, and now I wanted desperately to be a part of a loving and sustaining family. They didn't understand, nor could they realize the necessity of my departure. Tears rolling down my cheeks, I called them to me. This day could be captured in pictures, and I wanted it close to my heart forever. Rosie and Ramona were clutching the cuddly teddy bears I had given them the day before. I wanted them to have something special to remember me by, so I spent my last Bell paycheck for this occasion. Managing a smile, I put my arms around my little sisters and asked my mother to take a picture of this special scene. We were already an hour behind schedule, but it didn't matter. I would never again relive this moment, and Mother understood—as always! It was she who had demonstrated to me by her own life the price of sacrifice and commitment. Everything I had done the last two days echoed with the words "For the last time."

In our haste to arrive before the 2:00 P.M. deadline, we almost overlooked an important passenger—Sister Edwin, my fourth grade teacher. As my sponsor into religious life, she would sign me in on the community's register. We were to pick her up at 11:00 A.M., but it was 1:00 P.M. before we arrived at the local convent to which she had been assigned. There I was ushered into the study hall of the community. In the middle of the table lay several brightly wrapped packages addressed to me.

Brochure printed using Joanne as a model (second from right).

Unable to speak, I stared in disbelief. Extending their wishes for future happiness, each sister presented me with a package as a way of expressing good wishes. I was overwhelmed, and a captive of their graciousness.

After another round of hugs and warm wishes, we proceeded on our way. My head was swimming with the events of a day that seemed endless in surprises. With my two sisters in the back seat of the car, I chatted excitedly with Sister Edwin. Suddenly mother cried out: "Joanne! Quick! Hold Ramona's mouth!" It was too late! My darling little sister Ramona was expelling the entire contents of her stomach all over the skirt of Sister Edwin's habit. I grabbed the towel Mother always kept in the front seat and put it to Ramona's mouth. But the damage to Sister Edwin's habit had already been done. I couldn't believe what had happened! Calmly, my fourth grade teacher took Ramona, put her on her lap, and told us not to worry. The skirt could be washed. Little did we realize the trouble involved in this seemingly small task.

We finally arrived at the convent at 3:00 P.M. The sun was shining brightly as we walked toward the main entrance of the Motherhouse. Its peaceful surroundings seemed to encase me in serenity and protection from the sorrow, confusion, and frustrations of that memorable day.

Following Sister Edwin, we entered the building and proceeded to the parlor where the candidates were registered and admitted to the Postulancy. In the ornately decorated room with wooden panels, glossy hardwood floors, and elaborately decorated murals, we were greeted by a tall, extremely muscular nun with beautiful blue eyes. In a soft and gentle voice she introduced herself as the Mistress of Postulants. I was immediately magnetized by her awesome presence.

My father explained the reason for our delay. The Mistress of Postulants said that they had been anxious for my arrival, since I had been chosen to have my picture taken with three of the novices and two other postulants for a magazine, *Prepster.* The *Prepster* was religious pamphlet circulated throughout the diocese of Pittsburgh to encourage girls to choose this type of life. Having been selected for such an important display, I felt even more special and extremely happy. In years to come, I would proudly remember that beautiful scene of youth, hope, idealism, and holy glamour.

Returning to the building where I would live for the next three years, I was taken to a large dressing room where I was clothed in a postulant's habit. This shapeless uniform consisted of a wide black cape that snapped around the neck and fell from the shoulders in deep sumptuous folds, a long thick veil attached to a cap that covered the entire head of hair, with the exception of a front hairpiece that was permitted visible, and a long black pleated gown with long narrow sleeves gathered at the wrist. Habits came only in small, medium, and large.

A picture representing the four stages of preparing for the religious life. (Left to right) 1. Preparatory student, 2. Postulant, 3. Novice, 4. Final professed nun.

Since I was short (5 feet and 4 inches), I was clothed in the smallest size available. My appearance presented a picture of clerical authority and prestige. Its simplicity and religious connotation were a sharp contrast to the lovely taffeta dress, high-heeled shoes, and worldly wardrobes which I had formerly worn.

Walking gracefully through the hallway in yards of cumbersome material, I returned to one of the parlors where my parents and little sisters were waiting. They were so proud of me and praised me as I demonstrated my "new look." Pictures were taken of this momentous occasion. I was so happy. My long-awaited dream was becoming a reality!

As the time drew closer for me to say goodbye, I felt a lump in my throat and an emptiness in my heart. I was torn emotionally. I longed to serve God, and yet I longed to be with my family. I didn't really know my brother and sisters, nor had I spent time with them in growing up. Nevertheless, I reassured myself that I was identifying with God's specially chosen family. I believed that I would find all the answers to the needs I had longed for since my first departure from home—the need to love and be loved!

4
A Dream Comes True

"**D**ominus vobiscum" (The Lord be with you), chanted the priest from the altar. "Et cum spiritu tuo" (And with your spirit also), replied the community, their voices rising in unison. "Ite missa est" (Go, you are sent forth), came the priest's concluding words as the body of some five hundred religious chanted their final response: "Deo Gratias!" (Thanks be to God).

Kneeling in the pew with my fellow postulants, I felt I had just entered the gates of Heaven. The strong melodious voices held me spellbound during the entire Mass. As the nuns, young and old, glided to the altar to receive the Eucharist, I envisioned them as angels in disguise. A surge of impatience swept over me. How eager I was to become one with them.

At the conclusion of the Mass, the Mistress directed the postulants to the main dining room for breakfast. Seated according to age, I ranked 16th of the 21 newly admitted postulants. For the next 16 years of my religious life, I would be the 16th member of my group or "crowd" as each new group of postulants was called.

After breakfast, we were escorted from the main dining room of the Motherhouse to the third floor of the same building. This was known as the "Novitiate," and it was here that those in religious life were trained and observed by the Mistress of Postulants and the Mistress of Novices. The second floor was occupied by the professed members of the community (those who had taken their Final Vows). Neither group was permitted entrance into the living quarters designated for the other, nor was any type of communication between the groups permitted unless special permission had first been given by the Mistress of Novices.

As we climbed three flights of stairs to the novitiate, we were stopped by the Mistress of Postulants, who sternly reprimanded us for our frivolity. She informed us that strict silence was to be observed in this area at all times. That reprimand was but a taste of the rigorous training to come.

We made our way toward a large study room at the end of the long hallway. As we followed the Mistress of Postulants, I observed the stark surroundings which would be my home for the next two and a half years. There were four large dormitories. Each contained a dozen beds, six large cupboards, ceiling-to-floor windows covered by wide wooden shutters, and one small wooden washstand. This bleak setting was representative of the austere life during the period of religious training.

There were definite advantages to having lived the life of an aspirant for three years. Unlike the majority of new postulants, who were accustomed to worldly ways, I would not find the regimentation and austerity too different from that in the preparatory school. Within minutes these convictions were confirmed. Behind the closed doors of the large study hall, I would spend the remainder of my training days in this room learning how to pray, study, and grow in the ways of community life.

After assigning each new postulant a desk, the Mistress of Postulants spoke in a soft but firm voice. "Girls," she said, "from this day forward, you shall be addressed as 'Sister.' The Postulancy is a time of prayer, spiritual growth, and soul-searching as you pursue the religious life. For the next six months you will learn more about sacrifice and what it means to give up personal comforts. This will help you prepare for the dedicated service to which you will consecrate yourselves as religious. Your character will be tested, and, should it be determined that you are not prepared to live this type of life, you will be asked to leave the community. Remember, you have been chosen to be special servants of the Lord!" I listened attentively to the message that was being delivered. "I'll make it," I said to myself. "Whatever the cost, I am determined to succeed!"

During the following weeks, I learned the major concepts of religious life that applied to postulants. Since I was accustomed to rigorous requirements, I rationalized that I would be able to adjust to the stronger disciplines and more stringent rules in the novitiate. I was not, however, prepared for the testing that followed.

A short while later, a second meeting with the Mistress of Novices took place. At this meeting I was asked to surrender all personal belongings, including pictures of my loved ones. Photographs were considered strong reminders of the "old life"; dying to the world was my immediate concern. The memory of parents would pull me back to the world. This contact, therefore, was to be obliterated. Frozen by such a demand, I concluded that my superiors knew well the strong influence of family; thus the determined effort to break all such ties.

In addition, I would be permitted to own nothing. My possessions would become community property, as would anything that might be sent me from home. All actions were to be strictly monitored. Every movement from one part of the house to another would be controlled. Upon entering or leaving a room, I would be required to acknowledge the person in charge and request her permission to enter or leave. If late for any type of exercise, it was necessary to request permission to enter the room before the superior in charge, on bended knees, with hands folded beneath my cape. It was further required that I excuse myself and request a penance for tardiness. When passing another in the hallway, I was expected to say, "Praise be Jesus Christ." The appropriate response was "Now and forever. Amen."

The Mistress stressed humility in the development of the spiritual life of a religious. To discourage vanity, I was forbidden to use a personal mirror. Mirrors were displayed in the lavatories for general use. Were I to keep a mirror in my personal possession, I would be in grave danger of sinning. Such an offense was considered a matter for confession.

Since humility was high on the list of priorities, I was required to kiss the floor before retiring at night and on awakening on the morning. I was also required to kiss the floor whenever I was asked to perform an act of penance.

In conclusion, the Mistress of Novices impressed upon each of us the necessity for and the importance of strict adherence to rules and regulations.

I listened attentively, and I prayed for wisdom to understand the importance of the disciplines. One thing, however, troubled me. I could not understand why I should be deprived of the pictures of my loved ones. Questioning the logic and expecting to be understood, I freely expressed my concern to the Mistress of Novices. It had been my custom from early childhood to be open and honest with those in authority.

To my dismay, I received an unexpected response. I was told that nothing for God should be too difficult. My ultimate purpose was to become His bride. It was necessary that the worldly spirit be broken; hence, I was to yield to the directives. I was reminded that I was a prospective candidate to the religious life, and such stern discipline was designed to test my ability to persevere. The arrogance of questioning the rules resulted in my being put on penance for a period of several days. This punishment required that I be totally isolated from the rest of the community, including at mealtime. I was beginning to understand the community's interpretation of the term "discipline."

Later, in a private conference with the Mistress of Novices, I learned that the purpose for this action was twofold: first, that I might be humbled; and second, that I might serve as an example to the other postulants should they rebel against the rules respecting religious discipline. The Mistress explained that it was her distinct duty to observe my conduct at all times and to help me grow in virtue.

Although I wished to remain attached to my family, I was willing to forsake everything in order to please Jesus. Willingly, I tore up the photographs of my loved ones.

It seemed as if years had passed since I said goodbye to my family.

Nostalgically, I thought of people who were forced to endure separation for long periods, and I imagined the joy of reunion! We were permitted to write every Sunday and receive letters once a week, but we were only allowed family visits once a month. The first visit with my family would not occur until mid-October at the Autumn Festival. How I longed to see them.

The community sponsored a huge, annual bazaar known as the "Autumn Festival" on the Motherhouse grounds. Convents throughout the diocese of Pittsburgh were responsible for the operation of various booths, games, rides, foods, and crafts. The project not only raised money for the upkeep of the Motherhouse, but it also provided an occasion for friends, relatives, and community members to visit and re-establish friendships. I was caught up in the anticipation of it all, and I looked forward to the Autumn Festival.

Amid much excitement, I greeted my family on that brisk autumn Saturday. Mother was eager to learn of my adjustment to convent life. My father inquired about the rules and regulations of the community. Unable to confide the frustrations and humiliation I had suffered for fear of revealing privileged information, I assured them of my happiness. I bubbled with enthusiasm as I spoke of my forthcoming wedding to Christ and of my induction into novitiate life as His bride.

I laughingly recounted an incident that had taken place in the study hall. Some of the postulants had presented a play entitled "Snow White and the Seven Dwarfs," a spoof of the fairy tale. In the play we jestingly compared our roles in the postulancy to those of the dwarfs working for Snow White, alias the Mistress of Postulants. Chosen as the dwarf Happy, I influenced the other dwarfs to maintain a carefree attitude. When the time came to recite my part, I laughed uncontrollably. So much, in fact, that I contributed a little stream ending in a puddle near the desk belonging to the Mistress. Laughing and crying at the same time, I attempted to finish my recitation, but to no avail. From that day forward, I answered to the nickname of "Happy."

Completing my story, I assessed my parents' reaction. It was apparent that they were satisfied with my adjustment to convent life. It pleased them that I was happy.

All too soon it was time for them to leave. As we hugged one another and said good-bye, I determined that I would not destroy their faith in me. In essence, I was my family's ambassador before God, and I cherished the high calling of my vocation.

Days came and went, as did several members of the novitiate. Within a five-month period, four members of our crowd left the Postulancy and returned to their homes. Nothing was ever mentioned regarding a postulant's departure and return to secular life. Often the only clue was the removal of her personal silverware from the dining room table and her

empty desk in the study hall. Those of us who remained were bewildered. The silence of the Mistresses suggested that we should not
probe. Our role was not to question why, but to persevere daily in our
own pursuit of the religious life.

Work, study, and prayer made each day but a brief moment in the
span of time from September to March. My wedding to Jesus was fast
approaching, and the excitement mounted as I tried on gowns, sent
invitations, and rehearsed for the wedding ceremony.

When a postulant becomes a nun, she is dressed in garments representative of the community she has chosen. Our community had
chosen a dress style worn by peasant women in France during the late
1700s. To herald this glorious event, a public ceremony was held.
Gowns were borrowed from local bridal shops for those of us who
could not obtain our own.

It was necessary that the admission of each postulant into the community be formally approved by the Mother General, her council, and
the Bishop of the Diocese in which the Motherhouse was located.

Shortly after Christmas a priest known as the "Local Ordinary" came
from the Diocesan office to question us about our wishes to be admitted to the community. I remember the solemnity of the occasion when
I was ushered into the parlor to be questioned. Seated at an antique
redwood table, the middle-aged dignitary welcomed me and proceeded
to explain his twofold purpose. As the Bishop's representative, it was his
duty to determine whether I had entered the congregation fraudulently
and whether I was acquainted with the duties required of a member of
the congregation. I felt comfortable in my conversation with this high-
ranking official, and I assured him that neither violence, deceit, nor fear
of retribution had affected my decision. Later, the Mistress of Postulants
confided to me that the priest had been impressed with my astuteness
and the way in which I had conducted myself during the interview.

Though comfortable with the Local Ordinary, such was not the case
as I knelt before the Mother General and her council. Prior to formal
admittance, a conference is held with the postulant, the Mother General, and the Mother General's council in attendance. At this conference
official acceptance or denial of each candidate into the novitiate is determined.

I prayed fervently as I awaited the decision. Within moments, Mother
Mary Grace spoke in her confident and authoritative voice: "Sister, you
will be happy to know that the members of the council and I have voted
for your acceptance into the novitiate. We are pleased with the growth
and progress you have made during the Postulancy, and we believe that
you posses the qualities necessary to be a worthy member of our community. You have many talents, and we know that you will be a productive member of the community. We will be meeting with the Mistress of

Novices regularly for a review of your progress. We will be looking forward to meeting with you in two years, at which time you will be petitioning to take your temporary vows. Pray, Sister, that you will persevere in your vocation."

"God has spoken," I thought. I was honored to have been selected as Christ's bride.

Returning from daily chores one morning, I was stopped by the Mistress of Novices. "Sister, I would like you to come with me," she said. Taking me by the hand, she guided me to the large sewing room next to her office. It was in this room that the habits (a name given to the garments worn by religious) were made. Novices who were skilled seamstresses sewed the habits for prospective novices.

"I am going to try on your headdress, my dear," the Mistress said as she gathered the white linens in her hands. She continued "You will be taught how to make your own clothing, but for now everything will be readymade for you." I remember vividly the discomfort as she cut, pinned, and manipulated the starched pieces of white linens tightly about my face. I felt like a mummy being readied for burial. "My!" she exclaimed, "you look lovely!" I couldn't wait to see myself in the finished product.

In a few brief moments, my life flashed swiftly before me. Standing in the rear of the chapel awaiting the organist's cue, I experienced a lifetime of emotions. Now, at last, my wedding ceremony was about to begin. In a few moments I would be presented to the world as Christ's bride. My family and friends would witness this beautiful ceremony and proclaim my marriage to Christ. "I may be renouncing my God-given privilege to a man," I reasoned, "but I am being united in marriage to Christ, Himself!" This was a sacred occasion.

A resounding chord was the cue for the 17 postulants to walk up the main aisle of the chapel. As I moved slowly toward the altar, I experienced a sensation of weightlessness. The choir resembled angels as they heralded my arrival. Dressed as a bride, in a long flowing white gown with a soft veil covering my shoulders, I felt truly beautiful.

Looking up momentarily, I saw one of my young sisters waving to me. I tried unsuccessfully not to smile. Suddenly, a light bulb flashed. My Uncle Paul had managed to smuggle his camera into the chapel, and he had just snapped a picture of me dressed as a bride. I was delighted, though I knew that picture-taking was forbidden.

As the ceremony began, the Bishop questioned the Mother General as to the worthiness of the candidates. Being the official representative of the community, she declared us acceptable according to the guidelines prescribed by Canon Law. Following a few short prayers, we knelt before the altar. A long black cloth was draped over my white wedding gown, symbolizing my death to the world and my new identity as a nun in the congregation of my choice. As the choir sang "Veni Creator Spiritus" (Come Holy Ghost), I left the sanctuary to be robed in a garment that would distinguish me for the remainder of my life as a nun. During this time, the choir sang many beautiful hymns as we exchanged our lovely gowns for the simple habit of the congregation.

When I returned to the chapel dressed as a Sister of St. Joseph, I was convinced that absolutely nothing could surpass or even equal the splendor of that occasion. Standing in front of the Bishop, I was blessed with holy water, thereby proclaiming the sacredness of my present state. In a voice for all to hear, the Bishop announced the name of each postulant and the name by which she would subsequently be identified in religious life. "Joanne Howe, henceforth, shall be known as Sister Jean Raymond." Was I hearing correctly? I had specifically requested my brother Raymond's name as my first choice and my sister Jean's name as my second choice. I was thrilled that the names were combined! I knew my parents would be as happy as I. Joanne Howe would be identified as a new person, married to Christ and His church.

I studied the long dangling robes symbolizing my death to the world. The skirt, sleeves, and vest were made of heavy black serge. A white plastic bib worn on the front of my chest concealed any femininity. My headdress, attached to a small muslin cap which tied in the back, consisted of white linens worn across my forehead and fastened under my chin. An underveil of black cotton covered the back of my head, and attached to the cincture was a pair of heavy wooden beads which hung from my left side. This habit was to have special significance wherever I went. I was proud to wear it.

Immediately following the ceremony, I was permitted to visit with my family and friends for several hours before returning to the novitiate. How honored I felt when I read the guest list. My aunt, Sister Edith, and her companion, Mother Lucina (formerly the Mother Superior of the Franciscans where I had attended preparatory school); Captain Rose Kennington (former head of the Missing Persons Bureau of Pittsburgh); numerous aunts and uncles; grade school friends; and, of course not to be overlooked, my parents, sisters, and brother. One of the larger parlors was needed to accommodate all of my guests. How I enjoyed opening the presents: stationery, handkerchiefs, candy, stockings, and money! How I enjoyed sharing precious moments with loved ones! All too soon, I would have to say good-bye for a whole year. I dreaded that moment! Canon Law dictates that the first year of a novice's life be spent in silence. During this time I would have no communication with the outside world by letter, phone calls, or visits. Permission would be granted for attention to medical needs, but only in case of emergency.

With a mixture of tears and joy, I said farewell. I assured my parents that they would be in my prayers constantly. My family was the dearest

My father rejoicing that after six years, I am now a full-fledged nun.

possession I had in this world, and I would never forget their love and sacrifice. Yes, I would pray for them unceasingly.

Returning to the novitiate, I was handed the Constitution of the Sisters of St. Joseph. This was commonly known as the "Holy Rule." During the next two years of novitiate training it would be my obligation to study the Constitution and zealously apply its directives to my life. As I grew in the understanding of the instructions prescribed in the Holy Rule, I was to practice its teachings "in order to save my immortal soul." I prayed for grace to maintain its counsels.

After receiving the Holy Rule, we proceeded to the refectory (dining room) to partake of a magnificent wedding feast. The tables were decorated with bouquets of carefully arranged, fresh flowers. Each newly invested novice received an array of beautifully designed holy cards with memorable quotations inscribed on the back from other religious in the convent. Gifts given to me by many former teachers were piled neatly on a table.

This was truly a day for celebration! My childhood dream had finally been realized. I was now the bride of Christ!

5
Into Novitiate Discipline

A s I passed through the great door leading into the novitiate, I took notice of my new attire. The heavy black serge habit, starched white linens, dangling rosary beads, and a soft sheer veil presented an aura of sanctity and mysticism. I now possessed a new identity in name and appearance as well.

My mind feasted on the happiness brought by my family's presence at my wedding to Christ. What would they think now of the bald head beneath the heavily starched linens? I winced as I relived the agony of that excruciating moment.

Although I knew that my head was to be shorn following my wedding, this knowledge did not lessen the trauma as the barber's shears eliminated my curly blonde hair. I watched each lock fall to the floor, and I tried to comprehend the logic of this sacrifice. A woman's hair was her most important asset, and this I was to offer to God.

I discreetly glanced at my fellow classmates. They looked strange in their baldness. Embarrassed and self-conscious, I quickly secured the small white linen cap around my bald head. I would change this covering daily for the next 16 years, and I would shave my head at least every two weeks.

Now, as a newly invested novice, robed as a nun, I awaited instructions from the Mistress. As the meeting began, I was intrigued by her finesse. Her well-articulated words assured us that a cloistered existence for one year would be monastic in its discipline and spiritually beneficial. During this period I was to deepen my relationship with God through intensified prayer life and practice of the virtues of humility, poverty, chastity, and obedience. During this year I was to renounce the world and its trappings. This renunciation would include a weekly public admission of faults, bodily scourgings, discipline of the appetite, imposed silence, and seclusion from all secular and worldly influences. Only through these testings could my spirit be broken and my fleshly appetite be put to death. Only then would I be able truly to communicate with a God who had emptied Himself on the Cross.

My first year was known as the Canonical Year of the "Year of Silence," a period without communication with the outside world. I

A full-fledged Sister of St. Joseph.

would be taught the laws of the congregation (known as the Holy Rule), Canon Law (the governing law of the Roman Catholic Church), and the doctrine written for the Baltimore Catechism, which I would later teach in the parochial schools. I would become highly skilled and knowledgeable.

My ability to adapt to the rigorous disciplines would be carefully monitored by the Mistress of Novices and the hierarchy. They would determine the potential of each novice as a worker for the community.

I experienced a sense of inadequacy and frustration. Orientation to a new lifestyle and a new identity demanded psychological and emotional changes. Was God bringing me face to face with a self that needed such drastic change? Though perfection seemed unattainable, I determined that I would accept and endure all conditions.

The Mistress assured us that corporal penances and everyday acts of self-denial would serve to discipline us for a courageous lifestyle. Before completion of our first class, we were handed a steel tube with five inch chains attached to be used while taking the "Discipline." During this ritual, we were required to whip our bare buttocks with the chains and in the process chant a prayer called "Out of the Depths" (also known as the "De Profundis"). Such ritual had a twofold purpose: (1) To punish our weak and sinful flesh; and (2) To atone for the sins of all mankind. I later learned that this same prayer was chanted over the bodies of deceased nuns for their deliverance from Purgatory.

I glanced about the community and observed a common reaction: shock and bewilderment! I wondered whether they were experiencing the disgust and embarrassment which I felt.

A week after the shock of the "Discipline," we were introduced to the "Chapter of Faults." This mandatory weekly meeting in the Community Room required each novice publicly to confess her faults to the entire group. Any accusation against another could be aired at this time. Depending upon the seriousness of the fault, the accused was given a penance of saying prayers with arms outstretched, observing long periods of silence, or imposed absences from community recreation periods and general gatherings. This was perhaps the most effective way to foster humility.

After the general accusations, we were to confess our own outward faults (such as breaking the observance of the Holy Rule, committing sins of anger, gossip, impatience, etc.) and were then given a penance by the Superior in charge. If corrected, we were not allowed vindication, and we were to accept whatever penance the Superior deemed appropriate. While participating in the Chapter of Faults, we were reminded that this was an image of the last judgement, at which all faults would be revealed.

I was encouraged to subdue my unruly flesh by fasting. Bodily mortification required that I not only beat my sinful body, but also deprive it of food and sleep. I was encouraged to leave the table hungry. Being one of the youngest, I was frequently the last served. There was little food left on the plate by the time it reached me. Nothing in my past life had prepared me for these disciplines.

The first several months of the Canonical Year passed swiftly. Worldly desires dimished. Each day I faced a new dilemma, and each day I experienced the pain of change. That which was acceptable and normal in the outside world was unacceptable in convent life.

In the middle of novitiate training, I could take the restrictions no longer. I decided to return home. Tearfully, I appealed to the Mistress of Novices to telephone my mother. After a week of unsuccessful attempts to dissuade me, it became apparent that I was determined to leave, and my parents were summoned.

When I saw my mother, I ran to her in tears, and in her loving fashion she consoled me. Mother was confident that my problems could be resolved. She held me in her arms and told me about a dream she had had the night before.

There was a large farm situated within the confines of the Motherhouse, where dairy products were produced for five hundred residents. In mother's dream, a milk pump overflowed, creating an emergency. Activity ensued, and mother heard a frantic voice calling my name. "Sister Jean Raymond!" "Only Sister Jean Raymond can turn off the pump." I was nowhere to be found.

Although her dream ended with the problem unsolved, mother regarded the dream as symbolic. She felt the Lord had chosen this means to express His desire that I remain in the convent.

Moved by my mother's story and child-like faith, I decided to stay. Returning to the mother superior, I announced my decision to give it one more try. She smiled approvingly as she returned my Holy Rule book and expressed her care and concern for my spiritual growth. Her warmth and affection left me with feelings not previously experienced in the religious life. I later learned that the mother superior, in a letter to my mother, had expressed her belief that I would do great things for God and would be blessed abundantly because of my decision to remain.

Gradually, my days filled with prayer and meditation and deep study of Canon Law, the Holy Rule of the congregation, and the Breviary.

The Breviary, the official prayerbook of the Roman Catholic Church, consisted of liturgical prayers of the Church said three times daily with the entire community assembled. In the early period of monasticism, the monks prayed "Matins" during the night. In the early dawn they said "Lauds" (the morning prayers), after which they returned to bed. Later when they arose to begin their day's work, they felt the need for a common service to consecrate their labors to the Lord. They developed "Prime," which might be thought of as a second morning prayer. "Vespers" (the evening prayer) were said in the late afternoon, followed by "Compline" which was, in essence, a second night prayer. These hours of prayers, based on the book of Psalms in the Old Testament, were designed to provide a perfect way to consecrate the whole day to God. The Breviary set the spiritual tone and served as a means to sanctify the day's activities.

The first time it was my privilege to intone publicly the opening prayers for Matins, I practiced for days perfecting the voice, the tempo, and the rhythm required. Selecting the proper pitch and maintaining that pitch throughout the chant was a difficult exercise at 6 o'clock in the morning! Remembering that the external expression must harmonize with the internal spirit, I proceeded to Chapel, determined to be the best Cantor the community had ever heard.

As first reader, I was seated directly in front of the Mother Superior on the right side of the Chapel. As the leader, she intoned the opening prayer, after which I was to stand, bow at the waist in her direction, and answer her response. Awed by the privilege, I stood silent in the pew. I tried frantically to vocalize the words, but I could only whisper. The community stood motionless, awaiting my response. I felt a hand on my shoulder, encouraging me to repeat the response. With tear-filled eyes, I attempted once more to restate the words. Suddenly, they came forth with a remarkable resonance and clarity.

Following breakfast that morning, the Mother Superior stopped by my table in the dining room, leaned over, and whispered in my ear "You did a fine job in Chapel this morning, Sister." Her encouraging words and kind gesture inspired me for the rest of my years in convent life.

Life as a novice required concentrated study of the Code of Canon Law. I took a streamlined course on the essentials of religious institutions as outlined by the Code. This course encompassed understanding the dedicated life of a nun, the chain of command within the convent, requirements for membership, obligations for professed nuns, and the privileges to be enjoyed. It was necessary to become well versed in all areas prior to taking the vows of poverty, chastity, and obedience. No one was permitted to take the vows without passing an extensive examination showing that she understood and was capable of explaining the rules and constitution, as well as the doctrines of Roman Catholicism.

In the mind of the Roman Catholic Church, the religious state was viewed as one of Christian perfection. I was taught that religious life owed its origin to Christ himself, who, by His word and example, exhorted His followers to observe three evangelical counsels: poverty, chastity, and obedience. Rejecting the world's riches, Jesus of His own free-will chose poverty at His birth, in His youth, and in His public life.

By this example, Jesus encouraged poverty in His followers.

Born of a virgin, Jesus led the life of a virgin. Even His most bitter enemies dared not reproach Him with sin or imperfection. By this life, He sanctified the state of chastity.

During His short earthly life, Jesus practiced perfect obedience. Humbling himself, He was obedient unto death, even to the death of the Cross.

Finally, Jesus gave us the example of a common life within a religious community, because He lived in the company of His disciples.

Prompted by the teachings of Jesus, men and women seeking the goal of perfection, bound themselves by vows of poverty, chastity, and obedience. They believed that when Christ recommended the evangelical counsels as means of perfect love, it was His intention that these counsels be honored as vows. The Roman Catholic Church regarded the taking of vows as an essential step for the attainment of religious perfection.

In the third century individuals sought out the desert or other isolated regions in which to live in religious life. This gave rise to monasticism. During the fourth century, another form of the religious state developed: the "cenobitical life," or the "life in common." In the 13th century the great mendicant orders were formed. These groups of religious lived by begging. Finally, during the 16th century, and continuing to the present time, various groups of religious, having as their primary function to minister to the lay people, were established and approved by the church.

After I was introduced to the history and purpose of religious congregations in general, I learned the special purpose of the Sisters of St. Joseph. All religious are to implore God's mercy for the world by their prayers, retreats, and missions. Our community's primary function was to promote the welfare of mankind through the erection of schools, education of the young, and care of the sick. Through prayers and bodily penances, the Sisters of St. Joseph sought to relieve human misery.

The congregation with which I was now identified was founded in 1650 by Father Medaille, a parish priest, in LePuy, France. The original congregation of six nuns, all of whom were chosen by Father Medaille, grew in number to several hundred following the French revolution during the late 1700s. In 1836 six nuns were chosen to migrate to America and settle in the area of Carondelet in St. Louis, Missouri. This would be the headquarters for the Sisters of St. Joseph in the United States. In 1869 the Bishop of the Diocese of Pittsburgh invited the Sisters of St. Joseph to open a school in Ebensburg, Pennsylvania. The community and its teaching work flourished and prospered; thus the decision was made to expand in Baden, Pennsylvania. In this newly established Motherhouse, imparting instruction, Christian education, and ministering to the sick continued. Such was the original goal of Father Medaille.

I marveled at the courage and devotion of these pioneers. Impressed by the strong survival record of the Sisters of St. Joseph and thinking their endeavors pleasing in the sight of God, I resolved to prove myself worthy.

The time spent in the novitiate had molded my mind through study of the Code of Canon Law and impressed upon me the necessity of blind, unquestioning submission to laws. I was taught to love and cherish these guidelines and considered every act sacred.

I learned that our Holy Rule was granted pontifical (i.e. approval by the Pope in Rome) on April 26, 1948. In other words, the congregation was formally recognized by the Vatican in Rome, and its constitution would be preserved in the archives of the Sacred Congregation for Religious in Rome. This status granted special spiritual gifts of indulgences to congregation members who obeyed the rules and to their immediate relatives upon death. A plenary indulgence (the remission of all one's sins) was granted on specific feast days; on the day one received her habit and made Final Vows, and on the anniversaries of those days. These indulgences were applicable not only to the nun, but they could also be applied by means of intercessory prayers to souls in Purgatory. Purgatory was the state in the hereafter for souls having died in venial sin (a transgression of God's law in some slight matter) or with a debt of temporal (earthly) punishment unpaid to God.

In addition to the spiritual benefits of the Holy Rule, I was made thoroughly aware of the spiritual exercises prescribed by the congregation and the rules to be observed in the general government.

Because of the diversity of backgrounds and personalities, I could understand the necessity for harmony in our thinking and behavior. The Holy Rule provided the necessary rigidity to achieve and maintain control.

Not only did the Holy Rule require Discipline and participation in the Chapter of Faults, but we were to recite the Rosary daily. The Rosary was a string of beads divided into five decades, each made up of one bead for the "Our Father" and ten beads for the "Hail Mary." These were official prayers approved by the church. While reciting each decade, we were to think of an event or mystery in the life of Jesus or in the life of His mother.

Besides reciting the Rosary, we were to assemble on the first Sunday of the month for the "Conference." At this meeting, the Superior in charge pointed out individual faults and defects in front of the entire group.

I was taught that self-surrender was not a set of beliefs or morals. The self was to be surrendered totally to God through various works of penance and self-denial. When I fully surrendered, God would bestow His grace upon me and cleanse me from innate human selfishness. He would heal my sin-ridden soul. The paradox Jesus spoke when He said "Whoever loses his life for my sake, will save it" presented a myriad of conflicts throughout my entire religious life. Though I was clothed in the habit of a nun, Self haunted me as I sought avenues of self-assertion and self-glorification rather than self-surrender.

Obeying the prayers and rituals of the Church and praying the words in my Breviary, I toiled strenuously to surrender life, energies, talents, and needs to God. Daily I sought extra ways of communicating intimately with my bridegroom. I believed that walking through the Stations of the Cross (a ritual that is performed using pictures or statues while meditating on the death, burial, and resurrection of Jesus), saying the rosary, and mortifying bodily senses through fasting, flagellation, and imposed spiritual prayers and works would result in my eternal salvation. The thrill of dedicating my life to such a high calling caused me to pursue excellence in all that Canon Law required.

The vow of chastity called for the exclusion of all carnal pleasure, whether physical or mental. I would give up the natural privilege of motherhood. I was to refrain from any act contrary to the sixth or the ninth commandment of the Roman Catholic Church. I was not to indulge in idolatry or covetousness toward any person, place, or thing. I was to avoid idleness, dangerous reading, and familiarity with a secular. "Secular" was any person who was not a religious. I was not permitted to engage in sentimental or particular friendships with fellow nuns or with people of the opposite sex, nor was I allowed to be seen with the same religious person too often. "Particular friendships" were thought to have the potential for lesbianism. To avoid further closeness between nuns, total silence prevailed commencing at 9 o'clock nightly. This was known as the "Grand Silence." Breaking Silence constituted a mortal sin (a grievous offense against the will of God) and was to be confessed. When the superior rang the bell for lights out, I was not permitted to engage in any communication with another nun.

In keeping with the virtue of modesty, undressing in front of another nun was prohibited. Such an act was said to provoke impure and immodest thoughts in opposition to the vow of chastity. I was to dress and undress beneath the cloak of a huge white nightgown. The contortions I went through to unhook, unbutton, and unsnap my garments called for skill and endurance!

Such strict regulations caused me more confusion than ever about friendships. I longed for a friend who would sustain and nourish me and fill my deep emotional needs.

Often I would see two women walking down a secluded path, holding hands, laughing, talking, and enjoying each other's company. The next thing I knew, they would be corrected at the Chapter of Faults for displaying unnatural feelings. I decided never to initiate or attempt to sustain a healthy relationship behind convent walls. A deep personal relationship with another person existed only in my dreams.

I had been trained in obedience from early childhood, so the concept of this vow was not earthshaking. I was expected to obey the command of the lawful superior in all things pertaining to the rules of the congregation and the laws of the Church. Her word was law, and final decisions rested with her. I was not to question; therefore I was spiritually dependent upon her decision. The superior interpreted God's will for me. I was to forget my own selfish desires and aspirations. I was to accept every decision made in my behalf as ordained by God, believing that it truly was God who spoke through the superior.

I was to detest the spirit of independence and was to seek permission from the local superior whenever I did anything or went anywhere not within the confines of the convent. Within the convent, I was required to request permission to perform even the simplest acts, such as washing clothes, going to private quarters, getting something to eat, or using materials that not only belonged to the convent, but had been given to me as gifts. In seeking permission, I honored my vow of obedience and esteemed and preferred it to all other virtues. The act of obedience sought to diminish individuality and foster the virtue of humility.

I was to entertain lowly sentiments of self and, in a spirit of deference and submission, consider myself of lowly esteem, realizing my many sins, weaknesses and miseries. I was to consider it an honor to have the most lowly acts of work and position. By submitting freely to the opinions and guidance of others, I would fulfull my vow of obedience.

It was dangerous to explore feelings of loneliness, anger, fear, and depression. Feelings were undisciplined emotions. To exhibit them was a sign of weakness and a sin to be confessed at the Chapter of Faults. Faithfully attempting to maintain an attitude of humility, I ceased to be spontaneous and expressive, and became, instead, quiet and reserved.

The vow of poverty required that I renounce the right to own or dispose of any possession without permission from the superior in charge. I was to own nothing and waste nothing, and I was to exercise wisdom in the use of all things. Prior to taking my temporary vows, I was required to make a will disposing of any property which I might then possess or later inherit. The will would no longer be binding should I leave the convent.

Taking the vows would mean total surrender of will, feelings, and possessions for the sake of following Jesus. Total surrender! Was I capable of such unselfishness?

6
Temporarily Professed Nun: Poverty, Chastity, Obedience

*T*he months flew by as days became packed with study, prayer, and disciplined training of my will. Preparations were under way to test each of us for the work of the community.

One afternoon, as I was studying for the final exam in Canon Law, I was approached by the Mistress of Novices. She said, "Sister Jean Raymond, would you please come to my office? I would like to talk with you." I wondered what I had done to *meet such fate.*

As I closed the door quietly, the mistress said, "Sister, sit here at the piano and play for me." Nervously, I approached the piano. Why was I being asked to play? It had been over a year since my fingers had touched a keyboard. Would I remember anything from my eight years of instruction? But as if I had played only the day before I played one of my favorite pieces, "Fur Elise." Finishing, I turned to the mistress, waiting breathlessly for her comments. "Sister," she said, "we need music teachers in our community. I taught music at one time, and I am going to teach you how to give piano lessons. You will be responsible for teaching others this excellent skill. The money you make will be used to provide the local community with their weekly food and toiletries."

I sat there stunned as she continued: "I am going to assign daily practice time, and you will be graded on your performance. Always remember that you are fulfilling an extremely important service for the community in this capacity. Many local missions are depending upon your commitment for their survival."

Patting my shoulder to show her approval, the mistress gave me permission to leave, re-emphasizing the need to take this responsibility seriously. I left knowing that a new era had begun.

I remembered a phone call my parents had received years before from Sister Beatrice, the music teacher at Holy Rosary Elementary. She told my family that several pianos had been donated to the school and that a worthy family would be given one. Since my brother Raymond and I were taking lessons from her, and because she considered us promising students, our family was chosen. Having our own piano had increased our incentive for practice. Anxious to repay the church for this kindness of long ago, I determined to be successful in my new assignment.

Soon after meeting with the Mistress of Novices, our crowd was summoned for a test of academic ability to determine our eligibility to teach in local Catholic schools. We took the Scholastic Aptitude Test (SAT). Shortly afterwards, the scores were posted on the novitiate bulletin board for all to examine. Three members of our crowd failed to reach the requirements set by the community, a total score of 800 or more. They would be trained as cooks, laundresses, or seamstresses for the community. I was grateful that I had passed the SAT with the required score. My goal was to be a teacher, not a maid.

My attitude quickly changed. I was assigned to a month in the kitchen cleaning the huge pots and cooking pans for some 300 members of the Motherhouse. Somehow, the Mistress of Novices had heard of my adverse attitude toward menial labor, and had decided to teach me to appreciate cooks, laundresses, and seamstresses.

Several weeks later she called me to her office. Without any preliminaries, she asked if I had learned anything from my experiences. I replied that I had come to realize the importance of every assignment in the community for the functioning of the whole. She then informed me that I was being assigned laundry work for the remainder of my novitiate training. Seeing my disappointment, she assured me that these skills would be beneficial to the community and to my future. I was devastated! My whole body went limp at the thought of huge washing machines, laundry tubs, steaming pressers, and tons of white linens to be starched daily. I had never known anyone assigned to laundry duty who was not exhausted and unkempt. I stood there expressionless as the mistress reminded me of my need for submission and obedience.

The mistress reminded me that obedience and submission were the root and substance of religious life and the ideals for Final Vows. My duty was to serve, no matter what my interests or needs; and refusal to be subordinate would be a refusal to submit to God Himself. From that day on, I submerged myself in unquestioning obedience to every assigned task.

The ominous clanging of the chapel bells interrupted my meditation. The body of a newly deceased community member was arriving. The Mother Superior began chant with the recitation of the Rosary for the Dead. The community responded in unison with prayers for the repose of the deceased soul.

I shuddered at the community's custom for its dead. Since the disappearance and death of my nine-year-old brother, death had been a horror to me. I shied from entering funeral homes for any reason. To sit and pray over the corpse of a stranger seemed unbearable.

Before retiring, each novice was assigned to serve with another in an hour of watch in one of the parlors where the body was placed for viewing. I was scheduled for the 3:00 A.M. to 4:00 A.M. watch the next morning. Remembering the need to be obedient, I prayed for strength to perform that gruesome task.

At 2:45 A.M., a hand gently nudged my shoulder. Another novice whispered that it was time to arise, dress, and proceed to the room where the corpse was in repose. In robot-like fashion, I dressed hurriedly to replace the novices assigned the previous hour's watch. I wanted desperately to escape that assignment. I felt an eerie sensation. Everything around me was starkly dark and quiet. I whispered out loud as I moved toward the parlor and the death watch.

Entering the dimly lit room, I knelt on the cushioned kneeler to pay my respects before the plain wooden coffin. Looking into the elderly nun's face, I observed that her countenance was sweetly eased in death. The sign of her final profession—a thick ebony cross—was tucked between her stiff, cold fingers, as if to indicate that her ultimate goal had been achieved—eternal existence with her Bridegroom. I had flashbacks of my young brother's death. Grief and anguish overwhelmed me. Suddenly, a hand touched my shoulder reminding me that it was time for the two-o'clock shift to return to the novitiate for several more hours of rest.

Sitting next to my fellow classmate, I mechanically took up the recitation of the rosary. My mind wandered as I recited: "Holy Mary, Mother of God, pray for us sinners, now and at the hour of our death. Amen." As I prayed for the repose of that woman's soul, my thoughts centered on my own death. Would I lie in state, dressed in the habit of the community? What would be written about my service to the community? Would death be sudden or lingering? Would loved ones be present to grieve? How cold, impersonal, and insignificant these surroundings seemed!

Suddenly, I was shocked into reality as the corpse lifted abruptly from its resting place and gasped! Panic-stricken, I screamed and ran out of the room into the arms of the night watchman. Uncontrollably I cried: "That corpse is alive!" Hysterical and in a state of shock, I was led by the watchman to the second floor infirmary. I was sedated and put to bed in an empty cell. Later that day, I learned that the community did not believe in embalming their dead so the corpse contained and had expelled gases not released by the mortician. I was assured, however, that the nun in the coffin was truly dead.

Stress from that painful experience left me even more fearful of lifeless bodies, coffins, and death in general. Although I was teased about the "talking corpse," the authorities did not pressure me to maintain such vigils while I remained at the Motherhouse.

As a young novice, I looked forward to instructing others in the Baltimore Catechism, teaching them to learn and grow in the Roman Catholic faith and sacraments. The intense and thorough training in Canon Law, prayer, and Christology (theology on the life of Christ) was coming to a close. Soon I would profess my temporary vows of poverty, chastity, and obedience before God and the community.

The day for temporary profession rapidly approached. I could hardly contain my happiness. In preparation for that awesome event, an eight-day retreat was prepared for the 16 novices in our crowd who had persevered.

Of the five novices who had returned to the world, none was heard from again. I wondered what had happened to them. I had grown close to several during the early years of novitiate training. Pat had been a lot of fun. Unfortunately, she stayed in love with her boyfriend and found many opportunities to meet him outside the Motherhouse—at a drive-in theatre next door. One night, locked out and desperate at being unable to get back inside, she spent the night with him. We had been warned that anyone leaving the area of the novitiate without permission would be dismissed immediately. Later I learned of Pat's dismissal and deeply regretted her indiscretion. Another novice demonstrated impatience when corrected and eventually ended up "telling off" the Assistant Mistress. Notably absent from the group the next day, her lack of control and dismissal served as an example to the rest of us.

It was not uncommon for first- and second-year novices to disappear mysteriously from the novitiate. Usually, absence was noted at the dinner table, where her personal napkin disappeared. Under a veil of secrecy, she had been sent home. Then, at daily conference, we would be told that Sister So-and-So had left the community to return to the world. We rarely received an opportunity to bid Godspeed to a departing novice. The authorities totally destroyed our ties with the individual. I always suffered when any novice left, for I believed her soul was in great jeopardy in the world.

Several conferences were held on the causes of correction and dismissal. Prior to the taking of my temporary vows, I could have been dismissed for the absence of a religious spirit in my life, which could have caused scandal to others. If, after repeated correction and performance of various penances, I had not mended my ways, then the Mother Superior and her Council could have dismissed me. Should I have had, and fraudulently concealed, ill health prior to my entrance into the community and had the Mother Superior and her Council later discovered I had disguised my illness, they could then have dismissed me.

Acceptance into temporary profession depended not only on the community's vote but also upon the community's assurance that I would willingly and joyfully submit myself to its constitutions.

Throughout childhood and young adulthood, I had been obedient without questioning, and I believed that I would have no problem adapting to the stringent discipline modes of the community.

Several weeks before our eight-day retreat, I was given permission to see a local dentist about a toothache. The pain was unbearable. Once the Mistress of Novices realized the seriousness of the problem, she arranged for a junior professed sister to drive me to Ambridge, a small town 15 minutes from the motherhouse. It had been almost two years since I had traveled outside the convent.

I dressed in my finest attire. Each novice had received two habits at the time of investiture. One was to be worn during studying and daily chores, the other on Sundays, holidays, holy days, and while traveling. Everyday outer veils were made of strong black muslin that hid the black underveil attached to our white starched linens. We wore sheer black veils on special occasions. I was anxious to wear my thin veil to the dentist.

Feeling very dressed-up, I presented myself to the mistress, who granted formal permission for my companion and me to venture into the outside world. How strange it was to travel on the open highway! Riding along, breathing fresh air, I felt an invisible shield between me and the rest of the world. Nothing was familiar anymore. Faces of the people on the street seemed different. I felt that I had been cut off from life itself, as if life had been in suspension for two years.

At the dentist's office, I was greeted by the receptionist: "Are you Sister Jean Raymond?" Though quite sheepish and embarrassed, I still felt the magic of being called "Sister." After a thorough examination, the dentist decided to pull my aching tooth and substitute a partial plate.

I dreaded reporting the expense to the Mistress of Novices. I knew that once I became a temporary professed religious the community would be responsible for every medical bill, but would they pay a $200.00 dental bill? I wondered if I would be forced to ask my parents for money. I dreaded the thought, knowing their financial difficulties. They had paid the $200.00 dowry required for my entrance into the community, and I did not want to burden them with another bill. The mistress informed me that the community would accept this responsibility. She considered the payment of this bill as an investment, for they were depending on my future services to support the local missions. I reaffirmed my affection, loyalty, and love for the community, and expressed gratitude for their generosity.

Retreat day finally arrived. To emphasize the seriousness of the decision the 16 of us were about to make, the Mother Superior and her Council questioned us on our knowledge and understanding of the vows of poverty, chastity, and obedience. The temporary professing of vows would climax a commitment I had made at the age of six. I listened to the requirements of the community's constitutions. I had learned them well, almost by heart. Naively, I believed, beyond any doubt, that I would be equal to the challenges they proposed.

Finally, we were presented individually before the Council and interrogated about our motives and intentions. During this meeting, the Council determined whether temporary profession was being freely made without fraud, violence, grave fear, or deceit. At the end of the conference, the Council granted me permission to take the temporary vows. For the next three years, I could leave at any time should I not succeed in maintaining my observance of the vows.

Leaving the novitiate that morning, I was convinced that God wanted me to be His Bride, and that belief was confirmed through the Mother Superior and her Council. I was determined to give the greatest gift to God, who loved me so—complete obedience to my vows.

7

Into the Heart of Mission Life

"**I,** Sister Jean Raymond, do solemnly profess to practice the most profound humility in all things and the most cordial charity toward my neighbor; do hereby pronounce my vows of poverty, chastity, and obedience for a period of three years according to the constitutions of the community." Composed and confident, I spoke loudly and clearly before the whole congregation.

We souls in consecration to God made our commitments to our Bridegroom, Jesus. Because professions were solemn and private, only the community was permitted to attend. The celestial-voiced choir sang the "Te Deum," praising God for our great commitments.

Following morning Mass and breakfast, we gathered in the novitiate to await mission assignments for the coming year. My heart jumped for joy when I learned of my new assignment. In several weeks I would be teaching the third grade. Where? I was elated. I looked forward to living convent life away from the Motherhouse as a junior professed nun.

That afternoon we were permitted to tell our parents the good news. They were delighted that my first mission would be so close to home. Dad planned to call the superior of the local mission and express his happiness. My fifth-grade teacher informed me that I had been blessed with an especially kind, gentle superior. The parish was in an extremely wealthy part of Pittsburgh, and parishioners had always been cooperative and strong financial supporters of our community. I was happy that my first teaching experience would be positive and supportive.

Within a week, a large trunk was packed, tightly roped, and forwarded to my new destination. The convent, a large white Victorian house, was located in an old, established neighborhood of beautifully manicured lawns and well-kept homes. Years ago, I would not have given second thought to the structure or the landscape. Now I had a renewed interest, since this would be home for the next year.

As I stood admiring the rocking chairs that graced the convent's front porch, a small slender figure appeared in the doorway. With dark, expressive eyes distinguishing her stately presence, she greeted my parents and me graciously. As she directed us to a parlor just inside the front door, I glanced around at the decor. Shutters had been replaced with soft lace curtains. Flowering plants decorated beautifully carved end tables placed on either side of a magnificent Victorian couch.

Introducing herself as the local Superior, our hostess expressed gratitude for my assignment. I listened intently as she spoke of duties and involvements. I beamed with pride as she expressed her joy that I would teach piano lessons.

Anxious to see the rest of the convent, I said farewell to my loving parents. My foremost desire was to settle into the new environment. The Superior informed them of visiting rules for junior professed nuns. They could call once a week and visit once a month. I could not visit home for any reason whatsoever. It would be three years before this privilege would be granted.

Immediately after my parents departed, the superior escorted me to the community room on the second floor of the convent where she introduced me to the remainder of the community. I felt extremely shy and embarrassed as all six members welcomed me, each identifying her name and rank. Scanning the faces, I saw a mixture of joy, enthusiasm, sarcasm, apathy, and sadness. I concluded that, regardless of the environment or the people, I was there to serve God and live in obedience to His will.

Following this formal introduction, the Superior led me to my sleeping quarters on the third floor. I was pleased to be the only person occupying the quaint little room. Situated at the end of the hallway, it was the perfect place to escape from the day's activities. A large iron bed stood against one of the outside walls. Beside it was a tiny desk where I would spend hours preparing classroom lessons. A dresser and a small sink were at the far side. A highly polished floor reflected the room's simplicity.

Leaving my suitcase on the chair by the door, I followed the Superior to the first floor. Taking me by the hand, she guided me into the back part of the house to the dining room and kitchen. Those two rooms seemed extremely small compared to the rest of the house. I couldn't believe that they could accommodate seven people. Introducing me to another nun, the Superior said, "You will be expected to help prepare the daily meals, Sister. This sister will explain the procedure to which we are all accustomed. Dinner will be in half an hour, and I want you to start your duty today. Every member of the community has her assigned tasks: cooking, dishwashing, laundry, dusting and cleaning. You will also be expected to keep the music rooms clean. Any questions?" Saying no, and thanking the Superior for her kindness, I immediately went to work setting the table and following the instructions of the sister working in the kitchen.

Suddenly a bell tinkled at the far end of the house. Realizing that this was a signal for evening Vespers, I hurriedly completed my chores. I enjoyed saying breviary prayers and, tonight of all nights, I wanted to begin my new life with prayers in the chapel.

A convent chapel was a convenience the nuns appreciated. We did not have to walk great distances to the church building for prayers. Although we could pray elsewhere, having our own chapel saved time, and we could begin and end each day with a chapel service.

As the youngest in age and lowest in rank, I was assigned the front pew. The Superior always took the last pew and governed from that position. Though a complete stranger, I felt extremely close to everyone in that small setting. I hoped they would become the "big sisters" I had never had.

After Vespers, the Superior rose and proceeded toward the dining room. Lingering in the pew waiting for the senior sisters to disperse, I considered it good fortune to be in such a small mission.

Following dinner, the Superior took me to the school only a block away. We chatted about my new role. Taking great measures to encourage me, she gathered my textbooks and told me that she would help with the first lesson plans. "School is a week away, and we shall have plenty of time to get you organized," she said. As confident as she made me feel, I dreaded the first day.

A week later, I felt more capable and prepared. On the first school day, with a week's lessons planned, and a brightly decorated classroom, I was as eager as the students.

That first morning, something happened that would linger in my memory for years. About 11:00 A.M., as the students were busily engaged at their desks, one of the students suddenly bolted out of her seat and came running toward me. "Sister, Mary Jane is making strange gurgling noises behind me," she said in a frightened voice. I rushed to the back of the classroom. There, staring quietly into space, eyes glazed, a little blonde-haired girl was dispelling foam from her mouth onto her beautiful yellow dress. I quickly grabbed the wooden cross at the end of my rosary beads. Parting her lips, I inserted the crucifix between her teeth, then instructed a student to go to the office and call an ambulance. I was later told that Mary Jane had gone into diabetic shock because she had not received her shot of insulin that morning.

The Superior congratulated me for quick thinking and for remaining calm throughout this ordeal. I would always carry Mary Jane's teeth marks on my crucifix, reminding me of that first draining experience as a teacher.

Time flew rapidly as the school year progressed. Days were a frenzied rush. Starting at half-past five in the morning, I could dress in 20 minutes. After assembling for morning devotions and celebration of Mass, I went to breakfast and then to my assigned chores. Classes began at 8:30 A.M., but I had to be there a half-hour before the students' arrival. At

3:00 P.M., I returned to the convent, where I daily taught two or three piano students. On Saturdays I attended a nearby college, where I earned six credits a semester toward a Bachelor of Science degree in education, with a minor in music. The college assignments were difficult and required tremendous amounts of reading. Yet I believed that hard work was the most nearly perfect way to serve my Bridegroom.

Pressures built beyond human endurance. In February a severe sore throat developed into a flu-like condition that confined me to bed more than a week. Events during that illness led me to question the perfection of my state of being. Daily arguing by convent members resulted in bouts of loud screaming and shouting. I was appalled by the childish conduct of physically mature but emotionally infantile women. The lack of respect for individuality was reflected in speech and actions. I could not believe that a bride of Christ would stoop to such degrading conduct. I felt emotionally frozen.

The usual monthly conference did nothing to curb the gossip, slander, and daily tantrums. I was disappointed in the quality of human relationships. If a postulant or novice had exhibited this behavior in the novitiate, she would have been sent home.

Despite the tense, destructive environment, I suppressed my anxieties and continued the assigned duties. Surprisingly, I was treated with courtesy and politeness by the warring factions. That made me cautious of their motives. I retreated to my room during evening recreation or busied myself with household chores to escape the unpleasant atmosphere.

The school weeks passed quickly. My monthly teaching evaluations, written with flowery comments, noted that I was sincerely interested in the students' performance and over-all growth.

I was pleased that my students were learning and happy. My college grades were passing. I burned the midnight oil, ignoring the 10:00 P.M. "lights out" bell that announced the Grand Silence. Several times I was reprimanded for disobeying the nightly curfew. For days I would obey the bell implicitly; then, gradually, I would return to cramming and studying into the wee hours of the morning.

As a junior professed religious, I had extra chores added to my heavy teaching schedule: giving piano lessons, cleaning, running errands, and preparing dinner. Often, I found myself making up prayer time in the chapel after the other nuns had retired. I longed for the peaceful surroundings of the motherhouse. Life in the mission field was chaotic, and lacked the serenity of novitiate life.

The end of the school year brought utter confusion. An older nun left for the Motherhouse shortly after Easter and was never heard from again. The other piano teacher was suddenly taken ill and assigned to an indefinite stay in a psychiatric ward. With a skeleton staff to administer the work of the community and fill the vacant teaching positions, we looked forward to different assignments in the summer.

The junior professed nuns were to attend the first summer retreat at the Motherhouse. I was anxious for familiar surroundings and comfortable circumstances. It didn't take long to acclimate myself to the quiet and rest of the retreat.

In reviewing the first year of mission life, I concluded that God Himself had personally directed my survival. No one could have otherwise maintained her equilibrium and sanity in that environment.

I longed to share my frustrations with someone—anyone. The capacity for deep and close friendships had been starved out of me since early days in the novitiate. I had no one to talk to.

I dared not approach a superior for fear of rejection. I retreated to the chapel, where the tabernacle (the place where the body and blood of Jesus in the form of a white wafer were kept) became my main source of solace. Idealistically, I believed that being religious meant loving and sacrificing. Deep within my soul, I believed that life in Christ was one of peace and joy, and it could exist in religious life. I prayed that my new assignment would heal my utter confusion about mission life. Teaching was exciting and challenging, but living with unhappy, disgruntled nuns was an experience I did not want to repeat.

On the last day of the retreat, next year's assignments were taped on the doors in the junior professed section of the Motherhouse. My heart rejoiced! I had been assigned to a new mission on the north side of Pittsburgh! I would miss being close to home, but I would not miss the dissatisfaction and unresolved problems at my former mission.

That summer, I remained at the motherhouse teaching catechism classes at a local mission. I also took an extra class in college. On August 15, I renewed my vows for another year, and made plans to leave for my new assignment that afternoon.

Two other members with whom I had trained in the novitiate were going to the same mission. I was enthusiastic about being with people my own age, communicating with them during the school year. I was told that the Superior was relatively young, but very old-fashioned. Somehow this didn't concern me, since I would enjoy the companionship of others my own age.

Arriving at the convent earlier than planned, we three learned that the Superior was visiting the sick but would return within the hour. Exploring our new surroundings, we discovered that we would be occupying the convent's top floor. My cell would be a tiny room carved out of an alcove of the original structure. Opening the door, heat came blasting out and almost overpowered me. Even a fan did not dispel the musty odor that pervaded the entire third floor.

As we helped one another carry the luggage up the time-worn stairs, we laughed and joked about the antiquity of our surroundings. The three of us would share a common bathroom and a common hallway, which we would use as access to our private cells. In contrast to the former assignment, this convent was much older in architecture and personnel! Seeing the advanced ages of the nuns in the other cells, we were grateful to have one another.

Hungry after traveling several hours and unloading suitcases, we decided to go downstairs and visit the kitchen. Whom did we happen to meet on the stairs but the Superior? Smiling, she welcomed us, noting that we seemed to have found our way around the building. After a formal introduction, she told us that dinner would be served later than usual, and we could help ourselves to a snack.

Anxious to satisfy our hunger pangs, we were shocked to see a small tin of cookies in the center of the counter. There were only two cookies for the three of us, and the refrigerator was padlocked. We were told later that only the Superior and the cook could enter the kitchen. From that day forward, the three of us decided to have a small "canteen" in one of our rooms. We took turns monthly asking parents and friends to provide us with cookies, candy, snacks, and even sandwiches.

As the year progressed, I was convinced that my assignment at that convent would be the best in mission life—even if the refrigerator was locked!

I observed that several quite eccentric, older nuns cloistered themselves in their cells most of the time. The three of us had the run of the house. My days were filled with teaching, piano lessons, and visiting the sick. That year I was assigned to teach first grade, along with another junior professed nun. Together we organized and produced a dramatic Christmas program, incorporating difficult dances and choral arrangements. The accomplishments of our first-graders were acclaimed by parents and teachers alike. As usual, evaluations from the local Superior and community supervisors were outstanding and filled with praise.

When the year ended and new assignments were issued, I wept. I would be leaving my two friends. In many ways, we had broken the letter of the law by disobeying rules, ignoring the Grand Silence, neglecting to hand in food or money we received from home, and communicating with parents of our students on a friendly basis. Nevertheless, we had maintained our sanity and developed a close relationship. In spite of uncertainty about my next mission, I delighted in the memories of that year.

My new assignment allowed me to see an outlying part of Pittsburgh which I would otherwise never have visited—the Monongahela Valley. It would be in this valley that I would observe the realities of convent life and come to an awareness of sin among vowed individuals.

Once again, my parents accompanied me on an assignment and

provided transportation for the two-hour journey. It was exhilarating to enjoy their company again. What fun it was stopping at a restaurant and ordering my favorite meal—steak! Seldom did nuns enjoy such luxury! Our diet consisted mainly of pot roasts, fish, or casseroles—economical and easy.

The convent was impressive, with an enclosed porch surrounding the entrance. Awaiting my arrival on the porch were the Superior and her assistant. Welcoming us with hospitality unlike any I had experienced, they escorted us to the main dining room, where we were treated to mounds of food. I could tell by the treat that this Superior liked to eat! Also, she was quite short and extremely rotund.

I was permitted a final visit with my parents in one of the parlors provided for such purpose. As we sat chatting about the new assignment, my mother cautioned me, "Joanne, you need to be very careful with this Superior. Somehow, I don't trust her. Watch what you say around her." I was stunned; yet I trusted her judgment. Often she would recommend maintaining some relationships and withdrawing from others. She seemed to have a sixth sense about people. Several times I recalled strong disagreements with her, discounting her judgments. All too often, her predictions came true.

Listening intensely to her warnings, I prayed to always heed her advice. I knew she loved me deeply and was anxious to protect me.

Two other junior professed nuns arrived later that day, bringing to nine the total number of our small community. As I talked to them, I concluded that they would not be the kind of individuals I could confide in that year. I prepared for more loneliness!

One day during the first month of teaching second grade and first communion class, a student became ill in the classroom and was rushed to the hospital. For weeks she lay in a coma, her body wasting away from brain cancer. Preparations were made for her death. One of her last wishes was to see Sister Jean Raymond. I was summoned to her bedside.

Seeing a puffy, curly-haired child enduring so much pain affected me deeply. Although my own losses had been difficult to endure, I determined to be a source of comfort and strength to her mother. I can still hear her mother whisper, "Frannie, Sister Jean Raymond is here." Opening her eyes, the child smiled sweetly and reached to hug me. Amidst tears of despair and hopelessness, I encouraged her to get well soon and promised her a big birthday party when she returned to school. Several days after my visit, Frannie celebrated her eighth birthday in Heaven! That experience influenced my future work with cancer patients in the hospice program.

The Superior of a local mission plays an important role in the life of every nun. She sets the tone and atmosphere for everyday life. She not only exercises Godly authority but models spiritual maturity. As the year progressed, I became more and more suspicious as the superior of this mission displayed outbursts of anger and jealousy. Her physical and emotional relationship with a junior professed nun was outwardly indiscreet and was questioned by several senior nuns during a monthly conference. The Superior, accused of a romantic liaison behind closed doors, retaliated by refusing permission for the smallest request by anyone on the mission. Since she had tremendous influence on the hierarchy at the Motherhouse, no one dared cross her, fearing revenge. In fact, everyone pampered her, believing that was the best way to keep peace.

It was difficult to understand how an intelligent, attractive girl, like this junior professed nun involved could become so emotionally and physically involved with a dumpy, overweight, and homely Superior. Reticent to say anything to anyone, I also acted as if everything was natural and normal. I remembered my mother's admonitions! I also wanted to take my final vows, and without a good report from this local Superior, they could be jeopardized. Nothing would interfere with that goal!

May arrived quickly, and preparations were made for closing the school and finalizing activities. Cleaning, scrubbing, packing, and wrapping were the usual routine. I enjoyed the relaxation of the rules. Often, after a hard day's work, it was not uncommon for the Superior to rent an R-rated film and treat us to pizza. Many of the junior professed nuns on the other missions envied our privileges. Little did they know what we had to endure during the school year!

A week before departing for the Motherhouse, the three junior professed nuns were treated to dinner as a pre-celebration of our final vows. Each community member wrapped a little gift (some present they had received during the school year) and laid it on a specially decorated table. A large sheet cake baked by a local family was placed in the center of the table. Timex watches given by the pastor of the parish were laid at each place. We were taken aback by his generosity.

After three years of mission life and three years of conscientious study and strict training, I would be recognized by the Sacred Congregation for Religious in Rome as a full-fledged nun. That would be the highest honor bestowed upon me, and the greatest gift to the Bridegroom—my vows of poverty, chastity, and obedience.

8

Conflicts And Contradictions

Rain pelted heavily against the stone bricks. An air of somberness prevailed. Everything was in readiness for my final consecration to God on a dreary day, August 15, 1959.

Although this ceremony was closed to the public, my father attended because he brought my aunt to witness the final vows.

A priest asked, "Are you acting of your own free will to take your vows of poverty, chastity, and obedience?" Humbly I answered, "Yes." I was formally accepted by the community, with the Mother Superior and council in attendance. I pronounced the vows openly to all assembled, "to honor and keep the vows of poverty, chastity, and obedience according to the rules of the congregation and under the guidance of the superiors in charge." I also promised "to practice with God's grace the most profound humility in all things and the most cordial charity toward my neighbor."

Following this, the Mother Superior placed a thick, heavy crucifix (attached to a cord-like ribbon) around my neck to be worn openly on the breast symbolizing my complete dedication and final commitment to God. She crowned me with white carnations as a sign of victory. At the close, I was led to a small table in the chapel sanctuary. In a red-bound book, I signed a document entitled "Act of Final Profession," agreeing to the same commitment I had made when taking temporary vows. I was officially recognized by the community and the Sacred Congregation for Religious in Rome as a "final professed nun." Inwardly, I was not convinced that this was the way to serve God. I often questioned, "Is this the only way to be truly dedicated to Christ?"

During ten years in mission life, I was active in almost every type of service in the teaching field. As a music teacher, I was especially responsible for supplementing the weekly food budget. I also learned all the required domestic chores and was known as a zealous and dedicated worker. As classroom teacher, I had great expectations for my students and received high academic performance in return. A local television station, hearing about the Christmas performances I had produced and directed, televised them as part of their holiday programming. God had blessed me abundantly with talents in art, music, and writing, and I wanted to return them to Him as teacher of His children.

In January 1964, as a result of the Second Vatican Council, a question-naire arrived from Rome. It appealed to the superiors to renovate the lives of the religious in their communities. Two questions were poig-nant reminders: "Have you found, among your fellow nuns, superior, or others, help for your spiritual life?" and "Have you found true friendship in the congregation to which you belong?" To both questions I an-swered, "No!" I had never experienced true, unselfish affection from fellow nuns or the community-at-large. I had seen only an outward pre-tense of love.

—At one point, I believed that convents were diabolically satu-rated because of the constant abuses by those behind the walls. Frequent gossiping, backbiting, and cynicism proved totally repulsive.

—Witnessing this great lack of charity, I was appalled that those who were rude and uncaring toward others would partici-pate so nonchalantly in religious functions intended as praise to God.

Other questions concerned the attitudes of Superiors. Generally, they were too occupied with outside matters to attend to my specific spir-itual needs. They were too busy with "things" to share time and love with subordinates. Though I was supposed to reverence the superiors, to me they were fellow human beings, capable of mistakes and sins against God.

Many Superiors avoided conflicts by hiding behind closed doors. As a result, a "self-imposed" leader would emerge, assume a leadership role, and become an unofficial tyrant. Unfortunately I met one of these "pseudo" leaders during a mission engagement.

I first encountered Sister Bruce after arriving at the assignment. Her kind, soothing voice welcomed me to the mission. Beneath the mask was a tense, rigid, and spiteful individual with a sharp and cutting tongue. Her gossiping was constant, and people never knew when they would be maligned or destroyed.

I was fortunate to escape her tongue slashing. Because of her viciousness, I feared retaliation after I witnessed her in an embarrassing incident.

One night, after the "Grand Silence," I realized that I had not handed in the money from the daily piano lessons. I had left it in a box on the top of the piano, so I decided to go and get it. Money was to be turned in to the superior at day's end, and I was fearful of reprisal should this negligence be discovered.

Stealthily, I crept toward the music room. At the far end, near the piano bench, a door led to the parish's parking lot. Nearing the room's entrance, I overheard soft moaning and groaning. Curious, but determined to get my piano money, I boldly walked into the room. I stopped dead in my tracks! In the light I saw two undressed individuals seated on the piano bench, engaged in heavy necking and petting. Recognizing Sister Bruce and the assistant pastor of the parish, I excused myself, grabbed the money box, and left as quickly as I had entered. Tiptoeing hurriedly up the stairs, with pounding heart I closed the door to my cell and breathed a sigh of relief, then fell to my knees. With tears of shock, fear, and sadness, I prayed that the scene I had witnessed would not leave emotional or psychological scars and that God would be merciful to the two involved in the sinful act. Most of all, I prayed for strength should Sister Bruce and her passionate lover retaliate. But worry was in vain. For the remainder of that school year, I was treated royally by the two individuals. I did not disclose the incident to anyone, nor did Sister Bruce discuss it with me.

The turbulent 60s brought change within and without convent life. Ideas, theories, and counter-theories challenged traditional dogmas of the Roman Catholic Church and the authority of the Papacy. Dissident church members forced crucial changes in worship, national and local autonomy, morality, and doctrine.

As the renewal process began, many nuns questioned the validity of a system once looked upon as sacred and unchangeable that was now being swept with significant changes. Protestant hymns and folk songs were replacing the beautiful Gregorian chants. The Mass, the central act of worship in the Roman Catholic Church, was celebrated in the common language rather than in Latin. Saints, once honored and revered as heavenly patrons for specific intercessory needs, were abandoned by the church. Purgatory doctrines and the Catholic doctrine of revelation were refuted by church theologians.

Deeply affected by the identity crises erupting throughout the church and by conditions in society, many priests and nuns were outspoken against the church and for the oppressed and underprivileged. Intense feelings of indignation arose within the convents, and passionate outpourings for authoritative positions for women became a major church issue.

Many religious, bewildered by the drastic changes, openly expressed dissatisfaction with religious submission and questioned the church's structure and rigid conservatism. Radically changing attitudes within the convent highlighted the difficulties over the vow of chastity. They had entered religious life genuinely believing that this was the way of perfection. They now felt trapped when current thinking viewed that neither men nor women develop normally and happily if cut off from sexual relationships, that human beings are closer to God in contact with others apart from them, and that life without an intimate, committed relationship is less than complete. Even Catholic theologians were debating the value of celibacy.

The mind-expanding views expressed by church theologians took such a strong hold upon those in religious life that no one was untouched. I, too, questioned the dual values of convent life. I had never developed love or perfection through self-dedication to our vows. I had been taught that convent life was to depict agape love (Godly love in giving and sharing with one another through our humanity). The focus of agape love (a total abandoning of self for the one loved) was to be the total love for other community members. Once we abandoned "self" and sought only the happiness and fulfillment of others, deep and throbbing needs would be satisfied.

It was apparent, however, that the nuns I knew were preoccupied with their own loneliness, frustrations, and emotional starvation. This self-preoccupation caused many to withdraw into their own pains, leaving them empty and without love. Separation from family, isolation from society-at-large, and fear of illicit relationships with one another compounded the agony and loneliness in religious life.

After wrestling with conflicts and experiencing inward torture, I requested permission to see a psychologist. The Mother Superior approved. Both she and the council realized that I was not performing at my best, and they wanted to keep me within the community.

The psychologist agreed that community life contained many conflicts and contradictions. On one hand, it demonstrated to all that its members and services were dedicated to serving God and others above everything else; on the other hand, it was not meeting the basic needs of members or the world-at-large.

As sessions continued, the psychologist cautioned me either to surrender to the community rules or else consider leaving the convent.

Listening intently to his recommendation, I thought of the number of religious who had already become part of the "great exodus."

—Many had left because of lack of fulfillment, restlessness, or loss of faith.

—Some had left because traditional religious life was becoming modernized and updated.

—Others, mainly those affected by the women's movement, objected to society dominated by a male hierarchy and ruled by the Pope (a man) in Rome.

I was not out to change the institution, nor had I lost faith in God. Rather I desired to find the little girl who had never grown up but was finally maturing. I struggled with this identity crisis.

In June 1967, a bulletin was dispatched to the entire community ordering a change in the dress code of all religious. Two-piece suits were permitted, black or brown only. Traditional garb was also acceptable.

Irene, a personal friend of mine and parent of a former student, took me on a shopping trip to Kaufman's Department Store in Pittsburgh. It had been years since I tried on silk blouses, short length skirts, and lacy slips. Everything in convent life had come in small, medium, and large. The dilemma of selecting clothing size was embarrassing and confusing. Fortunately, Irene was quite understanding. After choosing the basic wardrobe necessities, Irene paid the bill. How blessed I thought I was! I had received no money from the Motherhouse for the initial clothing change, and I believed that God had sent Irene to provide.

During a weekly home visit, I told my parents that I intended to leave the convent. My father, having been in the same situation, asked whether I had sought a priest's advice and whether I had done some serious praying. He knew that, should I leave the community, those actions would be the requirements for the dispensation for release from final vows in Canon Law. I had done both. My mother was happy. Her motherly intuition had sensed my conflicts and suffering. She felt I was making the right decision. She desired my happiness at any cost, even if it meant leaving convent life.

Driving the 100 miles to my last assignment in the summer of 1967, I nostalgically thought of my first trip to a mission. How excited I had been, and full of idyllic dreams of the future. During those 12 years, I experienced the richness of teaching and had affected the lives of hundreds of children. They, in turn, had affected my life in many ways, and had taught me the beauty of child-like trust and love. A sweetly scented wind blew gently from the surrounding Alleghenies, easing me into deeper meditation. Pondering the needs of my soul, I questioned the voids in my life—not only the great spiritual needs, but also the need to love and to be loved in return. Would these voids ever be filled? It would be several years before I had my answers.

At early dusk, my sister Gerry, her husband Sammy, their two little children, and I arrived at St. Patrick's convent in Gallitzen, Pennsylvania. We were greeted by a tall, slender nun in a trim skirt and short-sleeved white blouse, with a touch of hair protruding from her short thin veil. I had decided to wear my traditional floor-length habit, though I was prepared to change into secular clothing.

There were four of us in this small mission. I would be teaching a regular fourth-grade class, teaching the choir, ordering and buying the supplies for the convent, cleaning and preparing the chapel for daily Mass, and teaching all piano students. From early morning until late at night, I gave constant attention to all areas.

I discovered that the parishioners were warm, generous, and hospitable. My relationships with them grew into friendships that I had never experienced in convent life. One of the women volunteered to teach me to drive. Another woman, a lay teacher in the school, took me shopping and helped me select clothing styles and patterns to complement my personality.

As the year progressed, I could see that the old religious lifestyle had become unsatisfying. I was restless and extremely unhappy. In February, after grappling with the decision to leave religious life, I called the Mother Superior at the motherhouse, requesting a dispensation for release from my vows. After discussing the situation and realizing that I was determined to pursue my goal, she directed me to request a written release. This would be forwarded to the Bishop of the Diocese of Pittsburgh. If approved, I would be granted a "Decree of Exclaustration." This decree would permit me to remain outside the convent and live life as a secular, but still allow affiliation with the congregation. The Mother Superior also recommended that I claim emotional and mental stress so that the release of my vows would be approved. I reassured her that I would not leave immediately, but would fulfill all the responsibilities for that school year. Several days later, I received the kindest letter from her, thanking me for all the years of service and expressing the hope that I would find the happiness for which I was searching.

Preparations for departure went smoothly. I wrote several public schools in the greater Washington, D.C., Metropolitan Area, because I planned to live with my brother until I was financially independent. My brother Richard had been with The Divine Word Missionaries from Conesus, New York, for eleven years. He knew what it was like to readjust to the secular world.

I received encouraging letters from each application, and, through the generosity of my sister's husband, and my dear father, I drove to Washington for a personal interview. I returned with a new job, a new school, and a new life ahead.

At the age of 32, after three years in a preparatory school and sixteen years in service to the community, I left my past behind at *1:00 A.M.* My sister Marcia, her husband, and three little children had driven three hours through a blinding rainstorm in reponse to my urgent call for help. My father, ill of Parkinson's Disease, was unable to drive such a long distance.

As I loaded the car with my meager belongings, I felt a pang of sadness and fear. I knew I was making the right decision, but I wasn't positive that God would forgive me for terminating my vows. Fighting tears, I hugged each one of the nuns and wished all God's blessings upon them.

The three nuns who had been with me in this small mission reacted with kindness and love. What contradictions I felt! Only at the moment of departure did I feel the genuine love and affection I had searched for all those years in convent life.

I received word that the person who took my place had to tell the parish priest of my absence. They said that the priest was in a state of shock when he learned the news. Only a week earlier, he had told many friends that it was his good fortune to have a talented, dedicated, and old-fashioned nun directing his mission. He had especially liked my choir, and he wondered how they would manage without me!

Leaving in the secrecy of night characterized my entire life as a religious. The world-at-large would never know of the failures behind convent walls.

Exhausted from the emotional trauma of my exodus, I sank back into the car seat. Though grateful for the experiences in commitment and responsibility, I had spent the greater part of my youth and young adult life in a system that was archaic in rituals, disciplines, and communication with the world. I was now entering another lifestyle that would demand commitment and responsibility as great as any I had known before. I welcomed the challenges of tomorrow!

9
New Beginnings

Readjusting to society was painful, slow, and initially quite confusing.

My first day at home proved frustrating. I struggled with the hurt and resentment in my father's voice and behavior as he welcomed me to the "asphalt jungle of life." I struggled with Mother's overprotectiveness as she suggested alternatives for adjusting in society. Overwhelmed by comments and solicitations, I pleaded for time alone. Separated from the family environment for years, I now felt suffocated by concerns and attention. My family relationship had been carefully and deliberately severed over the years and, like the rest of my life, would have to be built again, brick by brick.

Unable to cope, I spent the first night in a friend's home. Since childhood, Mary Ann had been a cherished friend in whom I confided my triumphs and struggles. There, in a neutral environment, I explored feelings of guilt and personal value.

I returned home the next day realizing that I needed time, space, and self-understanding to acclimate myself to this new way of life. I spent the next two weeks preparing for the trip to Maryland. My mother understood the kettle of feelings boiling inside of me. She understood that I felt pushed, pulled, empty, and anxious, all at the same time. She encouraged me to seek new adventures and opportunities, to look at the positive blessings I had. The Mother Superior and her council had given excellent recommendations on the referral forms sent by the Board of Education. I had received $200.00 from the community to purchase simple, ordinary things for survival. I also had praise and gratitude from the community for 16 years of dedicated service. After she recounted those blessings, mother admonished me for not trusting the Lord to direct my life. "God loves you very much, Joanne, and He will never abandon you. Never forget that!" she said. As always, I found her recommendations and solutions satisfying and motivating.

Before leaving for Maryland, I felt that I had to go to confession and receive the sacrament of penance (meaning sorrow for sin) instituted by the Roman Catholic Church. In this sacrament sins committed after baptism are forgiven through absolution by a priest, who then imposes a penance. So many negative feelings had invaded my heart since leaving the convent that I felt a deep need to cleanse my soul.

Once in the confessional, I began confessing my sins to the priest.

The Roman Catholic Church teaches that Jesus Christ gave the priests power to forgive sins when He said to the apostles: "Receive the Holy Spirit; whose sins you shall forgive, they are forgiven them; and whose sins you shall retain, they are retained" (John 20:23). It was important that I identify my position in the church, as well as my offenses, to the priest, who would either absolve my sins or refuse absolution should he discern that I was not truly penitent.

"Bless me, Father, for I have sinned," I began. "It has been three weeks since my last confession. I am a religious of 'final profession'." After revealing my offenses against God and "His church," I was given a penance. My penance was to say the Rosary daily for a week. Blessing myself, as the priest said "I absolved you of your sins, in the name of the Father and of the Son and of the Holy Spirit," I stood up, ready to leave the confessional box.

Suddenly, in a pleading voice, the priest said, "Sister, please stay a moment. I need to discuss something important with you." Alarmed by this unorthodox approach, I sank on the kneeler. He continued: "Sister, I can identify with the anxieties you must be experiencing because of your recent decision. You see, I am leaving the priesthood tomorrow, to marry a divorced woman." Shocked and unable to reply to this disclosure, I remained silent. The priest then said: "For years I have struggled with my celibacy, and for years I have avoided the real issues of life. I know now the meaning of love. I have no other choice than to leave a life of fantasy and facade. I have been living a sham. I know now that I need someone to love and be loved by; I need someone to come home to and be comforted by; I need to feel human and act human! Do you believe I am making the right decision, Sister?"

Listening to this frustrated soul, I felt extreme pity. In a sympathetic voice, I replied, "Father, I understand the fulfillment you are seeking, and I wish there were a simple solution to your problem; but in your case, the pain you may experience from such a decision may be more than the pleasure you will receive from marrying a divorced woman. We both know the church's teaching on divorce: divorce is neither recognized nor approved. You need to ask yourself if marrying this woman will be worth the price of your excommunication from the church. I realize you are grappling with a truth you are reluctant to obey; but, on Judgment Day, each of us must give an account for our lives as to our obedience or disobedience to God's truths. I wish you God's blessings in your decision. I believe you will make the right decision—a decision that will be the best for you in the end."

Without any further adieu, I prayed for both of us before the tabernacle, the receptacle in the middle of the altar in which the wafers containing the Body and Blood of Christ are reserved. (This solidly-built enclosure, built of gold, is kept locked. Catholics believe that Christ resides there in His physical presence.) I prayed that we would discover God's will for our lives.

In the following months, I would be totally unprepared for the explosive, emotional readjustments in a society with changed values and low moral standards.

My initial taste of freedom was most refreshing! I wanted to feel alive! I wanted to put my efforts into everything productive. Outside lay a whole new world of challenge and opportunity, and I wanted to grasp every worthwhile experience.

Predictably, my first involvement was in the Roman Catholic Church's Confraternity of Christian Doctrine Program, better known as CCD. I introduced myself to the parish pastor, presenting my credentials as a former nun. I requested membership and involvement in his parish. Delighted to have someone with my background join the ranks, he assigned me a volunteer teaching position in the CCD Program. After two years, I was hired to coordinate the religious training of some 300 public school students. In addition I instructed 35 teachers in Catholic educational principles.

Once a month, a training session was held at the diocesan CCD headquarters in Washington, D.C., for lay instructors. The roots of Catholicism were being battered and threatened by the dissident groups within the church-at-large, and it was considered necessary that religious instructors be aware of the constant changes. The hierarchies were doing everything within their power to thwart the radical movements.

Throughout those sessions, I sensed the gnawing disillusionment of the instructors. Fundamental issues underlying established worship, local autonomy, roles of the laity, family life, and the doctrine questioning the authority of the Papacy were being discussed and refuted. Reveling in the freedom of the 1960s, many believed that Catholics should have the right to decide troublesome issues for themselves. To resolve their frustrations, many lay people (Catholics who were not ordained as priests, who had not taken solemn vows as religious) were becoming involved in celebrating the Mass, in using private texts and unapproved prayers, and in manipulating liturgical texts for social and political ends.

The roots of this discontent could be traced to the deliberations and decisions of the Second Vatican Council convoked by Pope John XXIII in 1962. It was said that he opened the windows of the Catholic Church and let in a gentle breeze of fresh air. To my way of thinking, he had unleashed a storm of fury from an institution seething from 500 years of pressures and ensconced with archaic ideas, rituals, and traditions.

I observed that many Catholics desired an in-depth study of the Bible to replace the secularism and emphasis on social issues. They wanted more from their faith than what their church, their traditions, and their doctrines offered.

I could not help recognizing the disunity within the ranks of the church; the division between conservatives (Catholics who reaffirmed traditional dogmas and morals); progressives (Catholics who wanted the church to become more involved politically and more associated with the concerns of the poor); noninstitutionalists (Catholics who frequently refused to take seriously the teaching authority of the church and who occasionally, if ever, attended church services, picking and choosing what they would accept); and the charismatics (Catholics who had accepted early Christian practices, such as speaking in tongues and other miraculous gifts, and those who had incorporated Protestant fundamentalist practices into their prayers and liturgy). (All those forces combined to shape the modern-day Roman Catholic Church, affecting its doctrinal teaching.) The old traditional emphasis on dogma and knowledge gradually changed to an emphasis on faith. A faith growing from *experience* and *response* became the new focus of Catholic doctrine.

Amid the commotion and disturbances, my teachers were finding it difficult to nurture youthful consciences with the doctrines in the Baltimore Catechism. They faced a twofold challenge: (1) to make religion meaningful to a modern age without compromising traditions and teachings, and (2) to preserve the unity of church teachings in the midst of divisive issues.

One Sunday morning during a CCD class, a sixth-grade student appeared in my office doorway crying and exhibiting anger I rarely had seen any student display. Approaching him carefully, I asked him why he was so upset. "My teacher said my mother is going to Hell because she isn't a Catholic," he screamed. Realizing that his teacher was from the "old school of Catholic theology," I reassured him that God wishes to damn no one, that his mother only needed to believe in Jesus to be saved. The ecumenical movement had changed my thinking, and "situation ethics" (a situation in which the balance of right or wrong, good or bad, in any voluntary act depends on the total set of circumstances and probable effects of the act) had become my code of morality—even spiritual morality.

As significant changes took place within the Roman Catholic Church; so, too, traditional Western culture was going through drastic moral upheavals. Marriage struggled to maintain its identity. Bombarded by the 1960s symbolization of "freedom," some were refraining from marriage; others were divorcing. Out of this struggle came "free sex," "alternative lifestyles," and "free consciences."

My own tempered support and thirst for freedom were reflected in my dating experiences. Desiring to be independent and anxious to become emotionally fulfilled, I played a game of manipulation and exploitation that created havoc and interfered with my ability to be productive both spiritually and professionally. I plunged headlong into a frenzied schedule of dating to overcome emotional emptiness.

I first became aware of my femininity and womanliness during a conversation with a car salesman at a local dealership. Having finished a course with the "Easy Method Driving School," and having obtained a driver's license, I was eager to buy my own car. I felt confident and excited. In the showroom I was approached by a fairly young man who introduced himself as Dan. After some initial questions, Dan realized that I did not know the first thing about purchasing a car! Undoubtedly, my ignorance, naïvete, and vulnerability were highly visible. Anxious to close the sale, Dan questioned my credit rating and financial stability. Finally, in a state of embarrassment and exasperation, I told him that I had recently left the convent, that I had no credit, and that I was extremely poor. It seemed impossible to buy a car at that time.

Encouraging me to pursue every avenue possible for a down payment, Dan then asked me if he could take me for a ride in a dealership car. Believing his motive pure, and anxious to learn more about cars, I accepted his offer.

Riding in a new, luxurious vehicle confirmed my desire to own a car! Halfway through the drive, I suddenly realized that Dan had taken a side road. Stopping alongside a lonely wooded area, we engaged in small talk. Suddenly he pulled me toward him, kissed me passionately, and pulled at my blouse. I panicked and struggled to break free. I did not know him and had no desire to become emotionally or sexually involved. Seeing my fright, he relaxed his hold and attempted to calm me. Immobilized by fear and guilt, I begged to be driven back.

Apologizing and ashamed, Dan explained the reason for his quick, spontaneous advances. Married, and the father of five young children, he had recently discovered that his thirty-two-year-old wife was having an affair with a sixty-two-year-old man. With his ego crushed, he felt deprived and inadequate. Preoccupied with this indignity and loss, and desperate for companionship, he tried extra-marital affairs. Since I was everything he admired and respected in a woman, he had responded impulsively to my innocence.

Absorbed by Dan's story, and feeling tenderness for his pain, I rationalized that his infidelity was justified. I could not condemn him for attempting to secure some happiness in life, though I believed in fidelity in marriage. As we parted, I agreed to be his friend, available on a platonic basis only, whenever schedules would allow.

Walking home, I felt freedom and awareness I had never before experienced. Here I was, thirty-two years old, never having known the intimacy and pleasure of an emotional relationship between a man and woman. I had been a prisoner of religious upbringing and beliefs! I was willing to compromise those beliefs to avoid feelings of isolation and worthlessness.

I believed I could offer something of value to a male companion and that in return he would reward me with emotional support and a sense of direction. I did not know who I really was, and I thought it was impossible to establish a set of directions or values for myself.

In addition to Dan, I met other men through several dating clubs. As my social life increased, I monitored feelings and established a code of values that would have an effect on future relationships.

Drifting from one relationship to another, I learned that the one thing important to every man was sexual involvement. This caused great distress, because these standards were in direct conflict with my ideas of affection and commitment. I rejected the men's "animal calls" to participate in raw sex!

Despite doubts and regrets, I learned from each experience and worked toward a meaningful relationship that would include shared goals, emotional support, and positive directions.

Though successful in dating, I will still emotionally deprived and lonely. Attempting to avoid intense stress and spiritual starvation, I explored other avenues of self-fulfillment.

Through the friendship of another Catholic, I became a member of the Federated Women's Club. Using this as a means of fulfillment, I became active in the political and social workings of the community and eventually became club president—the only single women to hold that office. As President of the Federated Women's Club, I was involved in the state organization both socially and politically.

I also sewed clothes for soldiers at a local Army base, hoping to meet new acquaintances. I continued to use my talents as a musician, giving private piano lessons to friends and their children. During summer vacations, I traveled as a tour director with Continental Trailways. Through the urgings of my father, I saved money, purchased land, and invested in a home.

People liked me, and I made many friends. I received compliments on personal appearance, clothing, and the forthrightness with which I expressed viewpoints on world affairs. Immersed in the humanistic values of society, I found myself walking through a forest entangled with many deceitful, wrong pathways.

After four years of dating different types of men, I became emotionally involved with a married man. Tom was tall, dark-haired, husky, 35, and the father of one of my former student's. After 12 years of marriage, his activities and financial goals had created tension and conflicts between him and his wife. Her sense of inferiority had increased his desire for freedom and exploration. Tom had no intention of divorcing his wife, but wanted extramarital affairs. A shrewd, hard-driving businessman, Tom could acquire anything he wanted. Against my better judgment, I became one of his acquisitions.

I first met Tom at the scene of an automobile accident in which I was involved. Seeing me stranded and without any help, he quickly arranged to have my car towed away. Grateful for his kindness and thoughtfulness, I invited him home for a cup of hot coffee.

Sitting across the breakfast table from him, I admired his tenacity and single-mindedness as he described his material goals. Although shy in his mannerisms, he had a dynamic and vital quality that projected manliness and sexual appeal.

As we discussed his family and marital status, I sensed a gnawing dissatisfaction. Finishing our chat, Tom asked if he could take me to dinner sometime. Feeling that no harm could come, I readily accepted.

In time, an illusory and dangerous relationship began. I held on to my strong objection to participating in any type of sex. Because of the clandestine relationship I repressed feelings of shame and guilt that I was justifying consciously. I recognized the source of my pain: God's code of morality was stirring my soul. In the depths of my soul, I knew that God would hold me accountable for this sinfulness, yet consciously I tried to deny any responsibility to Him or His laws.

My days and nights were filled with thoughts of Tom. My waking energy was directed totally to the moments we could spent together. Arranging our encounters required skill, ingenuity, courage, and above all a capacity to remain alone for long periods. It is amazing that I survived a situation with so much stress and emotional havoc.

Following a year of depression, tension, headaches, and constant anxiety, I resolved to end the affair. The desire to avoid a serious emotional commitment had run its course. Without my knowledge, Tom was also feeling the pressures of an incomplete and nowhere relationship. Unable to release his pent-up sexual drives, Tom sought the companionship of another woman.

One evening enroute to dinner, Tom told me that he had a new mistress and desired to end our affair. Shocked and hurt, I asked to be driven home. That night, I rehearsed over and over the events of that evening. Unable to deal with the pain of rejection and abandonment, I reached for a bottle of Valium. I wanted to end my life. Without hesitation, I tried to swallow all the pills. Choking and gagging, I coughed up several, spewing them out on the floor. I was desperate and believed that this would relieve the grief and loss I was experiencing.

Surprisingly, I awoke late the next morning with a resurgence of life and hope. Somehow I believed I was a person of worth and value, but I felt powerless to withstand the emotional waves that had been set in motion. I knew that I had been totally unprepared for the devastating impact of the affair, but I also knew that I had untapped resources of help.

A teacher friend, Barbara, encouraged me to seek the advice and counsel of her friend, "a preacher of the Gospel." A minister of another faith? I had always been taught that salvation and direction could only be found in and through the Roman Catholic Church. Yet my anxieties were acute, and I was on the verge of spiritual and physical suicide. I needed the advice and help of anyone at that point. My friend arranged a meeting for the very next day.

That night I lay awake examining my thoughts and feelings. The person who had desired long ago to become the Bride of Christ had emerged into a disharmonious conglomeration of borrowed lifestyles with a value system that neither honored nor fit my religious beliefs. My Indult of Secularization had been authorized by the Sacred Congregation for Religious in Rome. It absolved me of any responsibility in maintaining my vows of poverty, chastity and obedience. But was I really free? Situation ethics was only an escape from personal responsibility to God's code of ethics. Before closing my eyes, I remembered Augustine's ancient words, "Lord, you have made us for yourself, and our hearts are restless until they rest in Thee!" The search for my true identity would be found in Him. How I longed for that experience!

10
The Search for Self-Identity

T he first time I visited a church not of my own faith, I experienced anxiety and fear. The counselor was a minister, a highly trained preacher of the Gospel. I feared that he would influence me and destroy my faith in Roman Catholicism. In any event, I knew that I had allowed myself to be seduced by the world, people, my feelings, and material possessions. I had lost my sense of identity and closeness to God, and I was struggling with a problem of "meaninglessness." I needed help!

As I entered his study, the preacher greeted me warmly, introducing himself as Paul Coffman. Inviting me to be seated, he offered to help me in any way.

Believing that this man could never understand my former life. I casually commented on my life as a nun, departure from the convent, and efforts to readjust to society. I told him that I was lost in a maze of confusion and despair, that I was searching for inner peace and happiness with men. In the hunger for self-assurance, I had lost the security of God's relationship, and I wanted to become reacquainted with Him in thoughts and feelings. I desperately needed to believe that God would forgive me if I was truly sorry and repentant.

Several priests to whom I had confessed my affair with a married man believed different consequences would result from that relationship. One priest, believing I was a morally good and religious woman, encouraged the relationship. He believed I could have a positive effect on the married man I was dating. Another priest, shocked by my behavior, depicted my place in Hell with such certainty and vividness that I left the confessional vowing never again to enter its sanctuary. I desired forgiveness and direction, not reproach and condemnation.

After listening to my story, Mr. Coffman reached for a book on his desk. Displaying its title, he asked, "Joanne, do you know what his book is?" Unfamiliar with the contents, but aware of its authority, I replied, "Yes, it's the Bible!" He continued, "My dear, the answers to all of your problems and anxieties are here in God's Word. The Bible will tell you who you are, where you are going, and how you will get there."

I was dumfounded! No one in my entire religious life had ever given me such a sense of direction. As a nun, I was not encouraged to concentrate on its contents, nor permitted to interpret it. The Bible was interpreted by Catholics in authority, and any in-depth study belonged specifically to priests and other theologians. My familiarity with the Word came primarily from stories in Bible history classes. During the Mass, scriptural passages were read from elaborately designed books on the altar, available only to the priests. As a novice in the novitiate, I was told to put a Bible under my mattress to ward off any demons that might tempt me during the night. I had taught religion and studied theology for years, but I had never studied God's Word for direction. I was totally ignorant that the Bible could show me how to be delivered from guilt, released from sin's slavery, and freed from fear of God's condemnation.

Leaving the church building that afternoon, I felt relieved that this crisis no longer seemed life-threatening. Although I forgot most of what the preacher had said, because of the anxieties of that first session, one statement left a deep impression: "The Bible is the answer to all your problems!" I questioned, "Can I really believe and learn its contents? Can I trust its message?" I decided that time would answer those questions. For the present I needed someone to analyze my problems, identify symptoms, and guide me in the right direction. I scheduled another appointment.

In the second session, I was impressed with how sensitive and observant Paul Coffman was. He saw me as a person who knew quite clearly what she did not want. He recognized a strong urge to free myself of self-defeating behavioral patterns, and he saw my commitment to survive. He assured me that this emotional turbulence would eventually subside, and that in time I would be able to cope.

At this point he began building my self-worth and self-esteem. Because of his many years of counseling, he could sense and recognize my need for acceptance, affection, and approval. He confronted my low self-esteem.

Sorting out attitudes, I realized that my entire adult life had been conditioned on three premises:

—To be accepted, I must reach a certain standard of maturity, attitude, and achievement.

—When I fall short of goals or expectations, I need to be pressured, shamed, frightened, or punished.

—I can regain the comfort, security, and strength I felt before I fell short of my goals and expectations in only one way: by becoming the center of my environment, by mastering my world, and by becoming my own god!

My sense of worth had been sabotaged by those unrealistic goals. I had not attained power over self and sin, or achieved perfection. No matter how many times I felt I had arrived, I was never satisfied. I was torn by failure and despair. Guilt, non-self-acceptance and lack of inner freedom caused waves of conflict within my soul. In desperation, I suppressed the conflicts, but the more I pushed them into the subconscious, the more these emotions betrayed me.

Time and again, I wasted emotional energy in warding off negative judgments. Under tremendous pressures, unable to grow, develop, and fulfill my true potential, I needed to accept myself the way I was—with *all* assets and liabilities.

In daily studies for six months, I learned that self-worth is based on five facts:

1. *God created me.* I was shown (in the Book of Genesis) that God made me into His own image.
2. *God loves me.* "For God so loved the world that he gave His only Son that whoever believes in Him should not perish but have eternal life" (John 3:16).
3. *God planned for me.* Psalms 139:16 states that God recorded every day of the psalmist's life before he was born. I reasoned, "Doesn't that apply to me also?"
4. *God gifted me.* Paul told the Ephesian Christians: "Each of us has received God's favor in the measure in which Christ bestows it," (Ephesians 4:7).
5. *Christ died for me and gave me value.* In II Corinthians 5:15, 21 Paul wrote, "He died for all so that those who live might live no longer for themselves, but for him who for their sakes died and was raised up. . . . For our sakes God made him who did not know sin, to be sin, so that in him we might become the very holiness of God."

I was not doubting self, I was doubting God! He had provided a way of escape from guilt and sinfulness with a priceless investment, His only Son, Jesus. In Jesus, I could have freedom from fear and release from a wasted life.

God valued me highly, yet remorse plagued my soul. I was painfully aware of my sins and continued to focus on the negative self. Fear of failure to reach standards of perfection and fear of rejection by God became the greatest barriers to a wholesome self-esteem.

One day as I listened to a song, "Amazing Grace," on a local radio station, I observed a common thread of hope woven throughout the verses, especially in the opening words: "Amazing grace, how sweet the sound that saved a wretch like me! I once was lost, but now am found, was blind, but now I see." Lamenting my deeds and longing for God's healing, I plunged into an intense study of His word.

Opening my brand-new Catholic 1971 edition of the New American Bible, I read notes on the origin of the Bible. It said: "The Bible is unique in that it had God as its author. The Roman Catholic Church derives all of its teaching authority from its tradition, the doctrines which have come down to it from Christ. This tradition is preserved in written form in the Bible, which contains the principle truths of faith taught to the Apostles by Christ. Because the Bible is so difficult to understand, it is to be interpreted by those appointed in the church as the official guardians and infallible interpreters of the Bible."

Closing the book, I asked myself "Do I know any Bible scholars?" I had heard many priests quote the scriptures, make references to complicated religious doctrines, and mention obscure names and events of Testament history in their sermons; but I had never heard any priest claim an in-depth knowledge of the Word.

Throughout the counseling sessions, the preacher quoted Scripture passages that comforted and strengthened my soul. The soothing words in Matthew 11:28, 29 assured me of God's abiding love and care: "Come to me, all you who are weary and find life burdensome, and I will refresh you. Take my yoke upon your shoulders and learn from me, for I am gentle and humble of heart. Your souls will find rest, for my yoke is easy and my burden light."

Anxious to discover other messages, I arranged a Bible study with Mr. Coffman. I was impressed with his knowledge of Scripture, and I admired his ability to quote passages accurately from memory. As a result of counseling, my self-confidence was strengthened, and thoughts and feelings became stabilized. Gradually, over a period of six months, a fresh, new self emerged—a more confident, relaxed, alert, and happy individual. I was anxious to see myself from God's perspective. I had been out of touch with God for a long time, and I needed to find Him and know Him so life could have real meaning.

Mr. Coffman (by now, Paul) was not surprised by my request. He knew I was genuinely seeking truth, and he was willing to guide me.

Paul directed me to turn to Jeremiah, chapter 29. Embarrassed, I fumbled through the pages, trying to appear knowledgeable. Seeing I needed help, he handed me his Bible, pointing to verse 13: "You will seek Me and find Me, when you seek Me with all your heart." Then he asked, "What does this passage say to you, Joanne?" I replied, "It tells me that God would make Himself known to me if I am earnest in my search for Him."

As we moved deeper into our study, Paul encouraged me to put aside all preconceived ideas and prejudices about God, His commandments, and the Roman Catholic doctrines. He stressed that I keep an open mind, that I pray for God to make His truths clear. I believed His Word was the authority upon which I would base my life, regardless of the conditions required. I intended to study God's Word believing what I could not see and accepting what I could not comprehend.

Study began with Genesis and the story of Adam and Eve. This suggestion annoyed me. I had taught creation and the fall of man for years. I knew the story well and was aware of its theological teachings, I thought I knew all there was to know about sin and its consequences. How wrong I was!

Paul asked for my definition of the word "sin." Quoting from memory the Baltimore Catechism's definition, I responded, "Sin is my willful thought, desire, word, action, or omission forbidden by the law of God. On account of Adam and Eve's sin (which is called original sin), we, his descendants, come into the world deprived of sanctifying grace and inherit his punishments." I then explained the two important divisions of sin as I had learned them through the years: "Venial sin (the evil that is done is not serious, and a person does not give full consent to committing the sin) and mortal sin (any evil thought, desire, action or omission that is considered seriously wrong, and the person involved gives full consent to committing the sin)." I was always cautioned to be on guard against the "capital sins" (pride, covetousness, lust, anger, gluttony, envy, and sloth), which were considered the chief source of all sin. Paul seemed confused by this lengthy explanation of sin, especially original sin. He then referred me to Ezekiel 18:20, where I read in the Catholic Bible: "Only the one who sins shall die. The son shall not be charged with the guilt of his father, nor shall the father be charged with the guilt of his son. The virtuous man's virtue shall be his own, as the wicked man's wickedness shall be his."

The words startled me, a conflict arose in my mind. I had always understood that every person enters this world with both sinful nature and inherited original sin. As a descendant of Adam, I not only was born a sinner, but was personally guilty and under condemnation before God. Before I read Ezekiel, I was unaware that I had *not* inherited the guilt of Adam's sin or the guilt of my parents, but had inherited both the ability to learn good and evil.

Turning to the New Testament, Paul asked me to read James 1:13-15: "No one who is tempted is free to say, 'I am being tempted by God.' Surely, God, who is beyond the grasp of evil, tempts no one. Rather, the tug and lure of his own passion tempts every man. Once passion has conceived it gives birth to sin, and when sin reaches maturity it begets death." "Amazing!" I said to myself. Contrary to all I had learned and taught as a Roman Catholic nun, God's Word told me that we must answer for our own sins, not for those of our forefathers. I concluded that Roman Catholic theologians were in error on that subject.

I was curious about Paul's choice of the story of Adam and Eve. As we reviewed their rebellion against God, I saw their fall in its entire perspective for the first time! I was not born totally depraved, nor born in sin because of their transgression. In Isaiah 59:2, I found that *my* sins alienated me from God: "Rather, it is your sins that separate you from your God, it is your sins that make him hide his face from you so that he will not hear you." I learned from Adam and Eve's drama not only the origin and problem of sin, but also the limitless love of God for His created. Because of His great love and tenderness, He allowed Jesus to leave Heaven's sanctuary and become man's sacrifice for sin.

For the first time, I understood God's response in Genesis 3:15: "I will put enmity between you and the woman, and between your offspring and hers; He will strike at your head, while you strike at his heel." Jesus would bind the power of Satan and claim victory for all who accept Him as their personal Savior.

My real problem became apparent. I was unacceptable before God and had a broken relationship with Him. That truth was verified in Acts 26:18, where God spoke of Paul's mission "to open the eyes of those to whom I am sending you, to turn them from darkness to light and from the dominion of Satan to God; that through their faith in me they may obtain the forgiveness of their sins and a portion among God's people."

My soul was heavy under bondage to sin. I wanted to give back to God the life I owed Him. How? I learned the answer while reading Acts 4:12 and I Peter 2:24: "And there is salvation in no one else, for there is no other name under Heaven given among men by which we must be saved. . . . He Himself bore our sins in His Body on the tree."

Reflecting on God's Word, I felt a restlessness and dissatisfaction with my life. Exhausted and fearing failure, I retreated from the battle for freedom until another day. There had been so much struggle in my life—so much change. Too many fragmented pieces needed investigation and clarification. I needed more information and direction from God's Word. "Tomorrow is another day!" I decided.

11
Coming to Grips With God's Truths

Paul knew that I was going through a "spiritual genesis." Anxious to help, he gently cautioned me to let God's Word lead the way. "God's Son came in the fullness of time," he said, "and in the fullness of time, God will reveal His will for your life."

Paul showed me several passages that gave me confidence in the Bible's reliability and guidance. "The Counselor, the Holy Spirit whom the Father will send in my name will instruct you in everything, and remind you of all that I told you" (John 14:26). "Your word, O Lord, endures forever; it is firm as the heavens. Through all generations your truth will endure. . . . A Lamp to my feet is your word, a light to my path" (Psalm 119: 89, 90, 105).

Paul stimulated my thinking with questions, shaking the bulwark of my faith in Roman Catholicism.

"Was Peter really the first Pope?" he asked. Secure in my knowledge of the church's teachings on the Papacy, I replied, "According to my understanding, Jesus appointed Peter as the first Pope. Peter then went to Rome and served in that capacity for 25 years. I have always believed that, beginning with Peter, the apostolic succession of the Papacy continued to this day. In fact, Matthew 16:18 supports that claim." Triumphantly, I turned to the Book of Matthew to prove my point. "I, for my part, declare to you, [Peter] you are 'Rock' and on this rock I will build my church, and the jaws of death shall not prevail against it."

"Let's look at that Scripture more carefully, Joanne," Paul said. "Jesus had asked the disciples who men were saying that He was. Some had said He was John the Baptist; some Elijah; others thought he was Jeremiah or one of the prophets. In Matthew 16:15 Jesus asked, 'But who do you say that I am?' To this, Peter, in Matthew 16:16 replied, 'You are the Messiah, the Son of the living God!' At that, Jesus said, 'You are Peter [Petros—masculine gender—in Greek meaning stone, pebble, or small rock], and upon this rock [Petra—feminine gender—a mass of rock —the truth that Peter had just expressed] I will build my church!' The rock (the true church) was connected with Peter's statement 'You are the Christ!' and its foundation was Christ Himself, not Peter. In I Peter 2:4-8 Peter himself declared Christ the foundation or rock when he said: 'Come to him, a living stone, rejected by men but approved, none-theless, and precious in God's eyes.' The controversy was settled when I read I Corinthians 3:11: "No one can lay a foundation other than the one that has been laid, namely Jesus Christ."

My conscience reeled. Throughout my adult life I had sincerely be-lieved that I belonged to the only true church, established by Jesus, under the guidance and direction of the Pope. Throughout the ages, history had revealed its strength, permanence, and unchangeableness through the Papacy. Through logic and reason, I had been convinced that most church doctrines were wise and holy; others I *accepted on faith*. Now, I was confounded with the scriptural teachings that the Roman Catholic Church was not founded on Peter, but on erroneous interpretation of the Bible.

As evidence disproved the apostolic succession of the Papacy, I be-came aware that Peter was a married man. Scriptures revealed that Pe-ter's mother-in-law was healed of a fever in Matthew 8:14, 15. Years later, Paul stated in I Corinthians 9:5 that "the other apostles had wives."

Despite liberation theology, I knew that the Vatican had relentlessly upheld the vow of celibacy for priests. The Sacrament of Holy Orders (when a man receives the power and grace to perform the sacred duties of the church) required celibacy the remainder of the priest's life.

There was no way to harmonize Roman Catholic doctrine regarding celibacy with I Timothy 4:1-2: "The Spirit distinctly says that in later times some will turn away from the faith and will heed deceitful spirits and things taught by demons through plausible liars—men with seared consciences who forbid marriage and require abstinence from foods which God created to be received with thanksgiving by believers who know the truth." "How could this be?" I questioned, "God's Word in no way upholds the doctrine of celibacy, whereas the Roman Catholic Church makes celibacy a test of faith and compulsory for all its or-dained priests."

Unable to reconcile these teachings with Scripture, I referred to the *Catholic Encyclopedia*. The section on "Peter" read: "A *tradition* ap-peared as early as the Third Century for the belief that Peter was the Bishop of Rome for 25 years—these years being from 42 A.D. until 67 A.D." That viewpoint had distinct problems. In Acts 15:6 about the year 44 A.D., Peter was in the council at Jerusalem. In Galatians 2:11 in the year 53 A.D., Peter joined Paul in Antioch, and about the year 58 A.D., Paul wrote his letter to the Romans mentioning twenty-seven Christians there by name, but never mentioning Peter (Romans 16). The Roman Catholic Church designated Peter the first Pope of Rome, though the Bible gives no proof that Peter ever went to Rome. The New Testament states that he went to Antioch, Samaria, Joppa, and Caesarea, but it never refers to Rome.

Though confused over the conflicts between my religious views and Scriptures, I remained steadfast in my belief that the Roman Catholic Church was the true church and that its teachings and traditions were divine and apostolic. I had been taught that the Bible *was not* a sufficient rule of faith and that God's revelations were also contained in *tradition.* Scriptures alone could not convey a sure knowledge of faith and morals. Determined to uphold my Catholic principles, I refused to believe that my church would teach me error!

Supporting the Council of Trent's position on revering all traditions relating to faith and morals, I maintained a defensive position. As resolute as I was, my friend Paul, stood more firmly, refuting my claims that God's will is found in tradition. He admitted that much of the New Testament came first by word of mouth; but the Holy Spirit saw to it that everything essential to mankind was finally recorded in the Bible. He said that the Bible does not undertake to detail all the exhortations and disciplinary instructions uttered by Jesus and His Apostles, but it gives everything necessary for salvation, growth, and guidance.

As proof, he showed me II Timothy 3:16: "All Scripture is inspired of God and is useful for teaching—for reproof, correction, and training in holiness so that the man of God may be fully competent and equipped for every good work" (NIV).

I gradually understood that the Word of God was all-sufficient to perfect every individual in the knowledge of His will as revealed through Jesus Christ.

Even Christ condemned tradition: "So—for the sake of your tradition you have nullified God's Word. You hypocrites! How accurately did Isaiah prophesy about you when he said: 'This people pays me lip service but their heart is far from me. They do me empty reverence making dogmas out of human precepts.'" Nothing could have been more explicit than the advice and warning in that passage. God will not allow His law to be mixed and adulterated with human tradition!

Even the Apostles used Scripture as their final rule of faith and authority: "See to it that no one receives you through any empty, seductive philosophy that follows mere human traditions, a philosophy based on the elements of this world and not according to Christ" (Colossians 2:8).

Christ said that the Sadducees erred because they did not know the Scriptures (Matthew 22:29) and, in John 12:48 Jesus said: "Whoever rejects me and does not accept my words already has his judge, namely, the word I have spoken—it is that which will condemn him on the last day!" I was confronted with a Biblical truth from which I could not escape. It was as if the Lord Himself had come down from Heaven to reveal to me the importance of embracing the Scripture as my only rule of faith! The Roman Catholic Church had long since departed from Apostolic teachings. I now hungered to know the doctrines of the true church—the church in the Bible.

Believing that Scriptures are the inerrantly inspired revelation of the will of God, I began searching more desperately for truth. I felt certain that the Scriptures would validate the sacraments I had participated in since childhood. In John 16:13 Jesus promised the apostles that the Holy Spirit would guide them into all truth: "When he comes, however, being the Spirit of truth, he will guide you to all truth. He will not speak on his own, but will speak only what he hears, and will announce to you the things to come. In doing this, he will give glory to me, because he will have received from me what he will announce to you." I reasoned that either that claim of Jesus was true, or else, as Roman Catholic teachings imply, the Holy Spirit did not complete what Christ promised! I intended to verify the fulfillment of Jesus' claim.

The most consuming and all-prevading influence in my life had been the Mass. It had been the center of my worship. In the Mass, I renewed my beliefs, acknowledged sins, implored God's mercy and forgiveness and petitioned for divine help to live a better life.

During the Mass, the priest, acting as the official representative of the people, ceremoniously transforms the wafer into the actual body and blood of our Savior and then offers it to His Eternal Father. I had been taught that, in the New Law of Jesus, there was no other sacrifice acceptable to God save the sacrifice of the Mass. The Mass was the same sacrifice as the sacrifice of the cross in that the principal priest and Jesus were one and the same victims.

How precious were the moments during the consecration of the Mass, when the wafer becomes the actual presence of the body and blood of Christ at the words uttered by the priest and it presented to God by the priest in commemoration of Our Lord's death on the Cross and as a sacrifice for our sins. This renewal of Calvary applied to the souls of all Roman Catholics the merits and satisfaction that Jesus earned by His death.

As a Roman Catholic, I regarded the Eucharist (Christ's actual body and blood) as the source of my salvation. At this solemn time (the moment I received the wafer), I was reunited in body and soul with my Redeemer and Savior, Jesus. The Council of Trent proclaimed that belief in the doctrine of "Transubstantiation" (the changing of the wafer into the real presence of the totality of Christ—"flesh and blood, body and soul, and divinity and humanity") was essential to salvation.

Since the Mass had been the most solemn and sublime act of religious worship, I longed to read the Scriptural passages establishing this sacred doctrine.

I thought, "I was told by God Himself that 'everything that pertains to salvation is identified in God's word' (II Timothy 3:16). What does the Bible say about the Mass, the act of transubstantiation and the repeated sacrificing of Christ for our sins?"

In Hebrews 10:10-14, I read: "And every priest stands daily at his service, offering repeatedly the same sacrifices, which can never take away sin. But, when Christ had offered *for all time* a *single* sacrifice for sins, He sat down at the right hand of God, then to wait until His enemies would be made a stool for His feet . . . For by a *single* offering he has perfected *for all time* those who are sanctified." Hebrews 7:27 states: "Who [Christ] unlike the other high priests, had no need to offer sacrifice day after day, first for his own sins and then for those of the people; for this He did *once* for all when he offered himself."

The idea that Christ's flesh and blood, body and soul, divinity and humanity were offered repeatedly as a "renewal" of the sacrifice of the Cross stood in sharp contrast to Hebrews 9:25-28: "As it is appointed unto men once to die . . . so Christ was offered *once* for the sins of many."

I had thought that the sacrifice of Christ on the Cross should be renewed daily; much of Hebrews refuted the idea of daily sacrifices, which are contrary to Christ's *one* sacrifice "for all time." In view of the Scriptures, I could not explain or justify the ritual of the Mass.

My heart pounded, almost bursting from my body! "Was this true?" I asked myself. "Each time the sacrifice of the Cross was renewed in the Mass, was the priest crucifying the Son of God afresh?" I wept. Still, I was not ready to concede. I was convinced that I would find support for the doctrine of transubstantiation (where the substance of the bread and wine is changed, but the outward appearance of the elements remains the same).

Paul encouraged me to turn to Jesus' words in John 6:54,55: "Truly, truly, I say unto you, except you eat the flesh of the Son of man and drink His blood, you have no life in you . . . for my flesh is meat indeed, and my blood is drink indeed!"

Grasping for hope, I said, "Doesn't this Scripture support the teaching of transubstantiation?" Paul encouraged me to read verse 63, "It is the spirit that quickens: the flesh profits nothing: the words that I speak unto you, they are spirit, and they are life!"

Not fully comprehending the meaning of those words, I decided to re-read the entire chapter. Deeply disturbed, I learned that Jesus spoke those words before the institution of His Last Supper with His apostles. In the last part of the chapter, I realized that Jesus was speaking of the spiritual eating of *His Word,* that through Him alone was life eternal (I John 3:24). When Jesus spoke of eating His flesh and drinking His blood, He was speaking figuratively.

I was shown other figures of speech. In John 10:7, Jesus said, "I am the door." In John 15:1,5, Jesus referred to Himself as "the vine." When Jesus said, "This is my body, . . . This is my blood," He did not mean for me to accept those assertions literally. I had often wondered how Jesus could have held His own flesh and blood in His hand and ingested them and still maintained His body intact. Finally, I learned that the Lord's Supper was a memorial of His death until He returned to claim His own. In I Corinthians 11:23,24, Paul outlined the significance of the Lord's Supper in worship. The Lord's Supper is a memorial of the death of Christ until He comes (I Corinthians 1:26). It proclaims the salvation accomplished by Christ's death and a message of God's forgiveness.

No Scripture indicated whatsoever that the real presence of Jesus was contained in the Eucharist. In the Acts of the Apostles and throughout the Epistles, I read of prayer, praise, and the preaching of the Gospel as the apostles' works with no reference to the work of celebrating the Mass! In Matthew 28:19, Christ gave an express command to preach the Gospel and baptize: "Go, therefore, and make disciples of all nations, baptizing them in the name of the Father and of the Son, and of the Holy Spirit," Nowhere were they commanded to celebrate the Mass. In fact, the word "Mass" does not appear at all in the Scriptures!

After hours of study, I began to understand the meaning and purpose of the Lord's Supper. The bread represents the body of Christ, and the wine, or fruit of the vine, represents the blood of Christ (Matthew 26:26-29; I Corinthians 11:24,25; Hebrews 9:14,15). Therefore, the bread and wine are simply monuments to Christ's body and blood sacrificed on the Cross.

I was totally bewildered! Many teachings, traditions, and doctrines of my religion were nowhere to be found in the Scriptures! My faith in Roman Catholicism was shattered by the revelations in God's Word. I knew that God cannot lie. Lying is against His nature. My studies were convincing me that there was only one standard of truth on which I could base my beliefs—the Bible.

For too long I had been deceived into believing that the Roman Catholic doctrine was exactly the same as the teachings revealed in God's Word. In Matthew 4:16, Satan attempted to overcome Jesus by misapplying Scripture when He took Him up on a pinnacle of the Temple and said: "If Thou be the Son of God, cast Thyself down; for it is written, He shall give His angels charge concerning Thee; and in their hands they shall bear Thee up lest at any time Thou dash Thy foot against a stone." Had Jesus consented to Satan's deception, He would have committed a sin of presumption, but He met the issue by quoting another text:

"Thou shalt not tempt the Lord Thy God" (Matthew 4:7; Luke 4:12). This showed me the importance of a correct knowledge of Scripture, lest I be deceived by those who misapply Scripture to support their own false teachings.

As I sat in my favorite chair late one evening, I suddenly realized what I had to do! I had been running from guilt; now I needed to be saved from sins and the penalty of death!

The principles revealed in the Scriptures would guide my salvation. I could no longer remain in Roman Catholicism, honoring its teachings and traditions, and still keep my commitment to accept God's Word as my guide for truth.

After 36 years of searching, I would, at last, be able to serve God by accepting His way of salvation and His truths for inner peace and happiness. I was excited about the prospects!

After four months of intense study, I finally asked Paul, "What must I do to be saved?" Leaning back in his chair, he smiled, "Joanne, I wondered if you would ever get around to asking me that question!" Speaking in a more serious tone, he said, "Why do you believe you need to be saved?"

Tearfully, I emptied my soul. I was a sinner; my conscience had convicted me of this. I knew that the penalty of sin was death. I was separated from the blessings of God. Outside of Christ and a right relationship with God, I could have no true peace or genuine happiness on this Earth, let alone reach Heaven. The teachings I had been conditioned to believe had left me totally confused.

I was willing to surrender my total life to God—my mind, my heart, and my will—not only as "a living sacrifice" to God, but in grateful response to Jesus, "who paid it all!" The power of God's truth was of greater concern than the fear of excommunication from the Roman Catholic Church!

Noticing that old attitudes of anger, resistance, confusion, and uncertainty were changing to acceptance, resolution, and submission, Paul sat in his chair totally amazed. Always low-keyed, empathetic, loving, and patient, he never lost his composure. For the first time, I sensed an exuberance and bubbling joy in his mannerisms, as if he was on an emotional high.

Removing the Bible from his desk top, he opened it and said, "Let's see how the Bible addresses the concept of salvation and what you have to do to be saved." He referred me to I John 1:5,6: "This is the message we have heard from Him and proclaim to you, that God is light and in Him is no darkness at all. If we say we have fellowship with Him while we walk in darkness, we lie and do not live according to the truth." Then he asked, "What is this verse saying to you, Joanne?" Summarizing the passage in three statements, I said: "First, 'men walk in darkness,' as this verse declares and my experience confirms. The darkness is sin and selfishness, which overshadows our entire lives. Second, 'God is light.' Unlike men, God has no darkness in Him. He is absolutely pure and spotless. Third, just as light and darkness can never live together, neither can God and sin. Just as darkness is dispelled by light, so the sinner is inevitably banished from God's holy presence; and he cannot have fellowship with Him until his sin has been cleansed away."

I questioned, "How can I, a banished sinner, be cleansed and forgiven so that I can have fellowship with God?" Once again the Bible answered my question in John 3:1-8:

> There was a man of the Pharisees, named Nicodemus, a member of the Sanhedrin, who came to him at night. "Rabbi," he said, "we know you are a teacher come from God, for no man can perform signs and wonders such as you perform unless God is with him." Jesus gave him this answer:

> I solemnly assure you, no one can see the reign of God unless he is begotten from above.

> "How can a man be born again once he is old?" retorted Nicodemus. "Can he return to his mother's womb and be born over again?"

> I solemnly assure you, no one can enter into God's kingdom without being born again of water and the Spirit. Flesh begets flesh and Spirit begets spirit. Do not be surprised that I tell you you must all be born from above. The wind blows where it will. You hear the sound it makes but you do not know where it comes from, or where it goes. So it is with everyone born of the Spirit.

Like Nicodemus, I was puzzled about the new birth. What did Jesus mean when He said, "be born of water and of the Spirit?" Then I saw that the new birth meant a spiritual change—a spiritual birth into a spiritual kingdom!

After further study I could have no doubt in my mind that when Jesus used the words "born of water" He referred to baptism. Baptism, I was led to understand, is both a burial and a resurrection—the act by which one is placed in (immersed) and delivered (resurrected) from water to walk in newness of life with God. That baptism involves the immersion of the whole person in water was further confirmed in Romans 6:4: "Through baptism into his death we were buried with him so that, just as Christ was raised from the dead by the glory of the Father, we too might live a new life."

For years I had taught that the sacrament of baptism was absolutely essential. The Roman Catholic Church allowed no child within its influence to depart from this life without being baptized. I was proud that everyone in my family had been baptized and was assured of salvation unless a member became guilty of mortal sin. Never before had it occurred to me to ask what scripture the Roman Catholic Church used to validate the sacrament of baptism and to identify the chief conditions of becoming a follower of Christ and a member of His church.

I read Acts 2:38 most carefully. It states: "You must repent and be baptized, each one of you, in the name of Jesus Christ, that your sins may be forgiven; then you will receive the gift of the Holy Spirit."

As an infant, I could not have believed, repented, or confessed Jesus as Lord, for I was not mentally competent to do so. Infants are born pure and holy. They have not transgressed a law and do not bear any transgressions of their ancestors, as explained earlier in this chapter. Jesus said of little children: "of such is the Kingdom of Heaven" (Matthew 19:14). To believe, repent, confess Jesus as Lord, and be baptized are commands to *mature persons* who are lost and in need of salvation. The attempts by my godparents to effect a spiritual connection between me and God were clearly unacceptable Scripturally. No one could repent of my sins for me, believe in Jesus for me, or be baptized for me!

I questioned the authenticity of my own baptism! Remembering that the Bible never contradicts itself, but reveals itself with clarity and simplicity, I carefully examined the Scriptures on baptism.

> The man who believes in it and accepts baptism will be saved; the man who refuses to believe in it will be condemned (Mark 16:15,16).

> Therefore, if anyone is in Christ, he is a new creation. The old order has passed away; behold, all is new! (II Corinthians 5:17).

> All of you who have been baptized into Christ have clothed yourselves with him (Galatians 3:27).

> In baptism you were not only buried with him but also raised to life with him because you believed in the power of God who raised him from the dead (Colossians 2:12).

> You are now saved by a baptismal bath which corresponds to this exactly. This baptism is no removal of physical stain, but the pledge to God of an irreproachable conscience through the resurrection of Jesus Christ (I Peter 3:21).

> Are you not aware that we who were baptized into Christ Jesus were baptized into his death? Through baptism into his death we were buried with him, so that, just as Christ was raised from the dead by the glory of the Father, we too might live a new life. If we have been united with him through likeness to his death, so shall we be through a like resurrection (Romans 6:3-5).

According to the Bible, it was clear that Jesus placed both faith and baptism before salvation. Baptism was the means appointed by God for the "new birth." When one is born of the Spirit, the heart is regenerated following baptism with new and holy principles of life, with the love of sin abandoned. This process begins when the Gospel is preached and the hearer believes. Confessing that Jesus is Lord and Savior, the penitent believer is immersed in the water of baptism to walk from the kingdom of Satan (the world) into the kingdom of Christ (the church) that Jesus said He would build (Matthew 16:18), and to which He added "those who were being saved" (Acts 2:47).

These revelations were all so new! I would not be whole until I entered into Christ. To join Him, I would have to come in contact with His blood. Only baptism (no other provision) is the means by which a person can get "into Christ." In view of all I had read, I knew I had to make a decision. I weighed that knowledge heavily, and counted the cost.

I had always been sincere about serving God; but I was learning that God required more than sincerity. Proverbs 14:12 states, "There is a way that seemeth right unto a man, but the end thereof is the way of death."

I had been convinced before that I was worshiping God in an acceptable way. My new studies now taught me that my way was not God's way and that it would lead to death. In Romans 10:1-2, the apostle Paul said: "Brothers, my heart's desire, my prayer to God for the Israelites is that they may be saved. Indeed, I testify that they are zealous for God though their zeal is unenlightened." Just being religious was insufficient in God's eyes. I prayed for strength to obey His commands and submit to His will.

For weeks I had alternated between Sunday services at the Catholic Church and the worship services at Paul's congregation. I was always impressed by the quiet, pleasantly uplifting manner in which the services were conducted.

The concept of worshiping in the way of the early church was so foreign to me! I had been used to rote prayers; in this new worship service I heard spontaneous prayer from the heart. The singing was unbelievably beautiful and inspiring! As a former choir teacher, I had listened to resounding organ music mingled with the almost inaudible voices of the choir and those attending Mass. In this new experience, I was enjoying an entire congregation singing *a cappella* and harmonizing in four parts. The songs that were sung praised God, encouraged and exhorted God's people, and expanded their thinking upon His Word.

The simplicity of the Lord's Supper was deeply touching. There were no chimes rung nor specific words spoken to announce any dramatic moment! There was no mysticism or awesomeness displayed over the breaking of the bread. It was merely the response of love and appreciation to the simple command that Jesus gave at the Last Supper: "Do this in remembrance of me."

I had a difficult time adjusting to this new type of worship service! How was I to respond in a service in which the entire congregation participated?

I learned that every action in the service was patterned after the way in which the first century Christians worshiped. They contributed of their means on the first day of each week as they had prospered (I Corinthians 16:1,2). The early Christians were exhorted to prepare for the day when they would be with God, which would be their reward for persevering in the faith and for sharing the message of salvation (I Corinthians 3:8; Colossians 3:24; Hebrews 10:35,36).

The more I participated in the worship service with that group of people, the closer God seemed. I was finding spiritual strength unlike anything I had experienced during my participation in the Mass. Spiritual needs were being addressed by the power of the Gospel, "a two-edged sword" cutting to the marrow of my bones. Each time I heard the invitation call to come forward (an opportunity for those who desired to repent), I became painfully aware of my sins and estrangement from God. God was pursuing me, and I was trying desperately to elude Him.

I had broken out of one "habit," and I shuddered at the thought of putting on another! So many acts and habits of worship had become crystallized and hardened into a pattern by years of twisted thinking, reactions, and responses. Could I abandon life-long habits of saying the rosary, making novenas, attending Mass, venerating the saints, praying to Mary, and confessing my sins to a priest?

One Sunday evening after the worship service, I was invited to attend a fellowship in honor of a member of the congregation who was leaving the area. While I was enjoying myself in the fellowship hall, Paul sat down beside me and started talking. Suddenly, out of the clear blue, he said, "Joanne, you know the truth of the Gospel! Why won't you accept it?" He caught me off guard. I remember looking at him and feeling angry, self-conscious, hurt, and frustrated. Then, almost at the point of tears, my words tumbled out:

"Paul, you know what I've been through! You know that, for 19 years I gave my life and made a total commitment to that which I sincerely believed was God's design for me in this life, so I could be happy with God for all eternity. Yes, I now know God's plan for salvation, but my heart and will are not ready to make the commitment God requires! If I ever do decide to make that commitment and take that step, I want to be perfectly sure that I will not turn back."

I went home disturbed and unhappy!

12

Surrender to God's Will

O ctober 4, 1972, will long be remembered as my day of liberation. I arose early that morning, anxious to begin the day with an hour of study in God's Word and a brisk morning walk. Later, I would worship with New Testament Christians with whom I had been meeting on Sunday and Wednesday evenings.

My Bible study that particular day centered on the Book of Hebrews and the Law. Paul Coffman and I had had many stirring conversations about the Ten Commandments and whether they apply today. I contended that God gave Israel the Ten Commandments as His Supreme Law of righteousness and that that Law is in force today. Paul's position was that God gave the children of Israel the Law of Moses to govern them until the coming of Christ—to serve as a schoolmaster leading them to Christ (Galatians 3:24). He had explained the meaning of "covenant," an agreement or contract between two or more parties.

In one of our studies, I learned that the first covenant (also called the Old Covenant) was made with Abraham. Genesis 12:1-7 states that God promised Abraham to make of him a great nation, blessing those who blessed Abraham and cursing those who cursed Abraham. In Abraham's seed (descendants) he would also bless all of the nations of the earth. Circumcision was a sign of that agreement. That covenant was not put in written form until it was repeated in the Law of Moses.

The Law of Moses restated the promises and added regulations. I was shown in Exodus 34:27-28 that God said that the Ten Commandments, written on tables of stone, were a covenant with Moses and with Israel. The Law of Moses, Paul explained, was therefore given only to the Jews, and lasted only until the death of Christ. It was a law of the letter rather than the Spirit, and was sealed by the blood of animal sacrifices.

Paul asked me to read the Book of Hebrews, challenging me to uphold my belief that we were to obey the Ten Commandments given to Moses.

Eager to respond to a reasonable challenge, I plunged headlong into a study of Hebrews. I sensed my position was extremely weak, but I was determined to find some Scriptures supporting my thinking. After all, the Catholic Church could not have erred in *this* teaching all of these years!

The more I studied Hebrews, the more I uncovered evidence that Jesus' death fulfilled the Old Covenant, and that a new Covenant (or second covenant) had been established between God and man. Hebrews 8:6-8, 13 confirmed that fact: "But, as it is, Jesus has obtained a more excellent ministry now, just as he is mediator of a better covenant, founded on better promises. If that first covenant had been faultless, there would have been no place for a second one." When God says "a new covenant," He declares the first one obsolete.

"So, Paul was right," I sighed. God's Word had told me that the New Covenant is better than the old and far more important for us today. Jesus, as the seed of Abraham, has blessed all mankind by making salvation possible through His shed blood on the Cross.

The more I read, the more I realized how inferior and incomplete was the Law of Moses—the Ten Commandments. Under the Old Covenant, the law revealed the enormity of sin and was a *legal* standard for man's guidance; however, God's people used it as a means of self-justification and merit-earning. God never intended for the Law to bring salvation; salvation is the result of *grace.*

After identifying those overwhelming differences, I concluded:

In His death, Jesus fulfilled the Law, as taught in Matthew 5:17: "Think not that I am come to destroy the law, or the prophets. I am not come to destroy, but to fulfill."

The apostle Paul established the replacement of the Old for the New when he said: "Wherefore, my brethren, you also are become dead to the law by the body of Christ . . . but now we are delivered from the Law, that being dead wherein we were held that we should serve in newness of the Spirit, and not in the oldness of the Letter" (Romans 7:4, 6).

In Colossians 2:14, Paul wrote: "Christ cancelled the Law of Moses that stood against us with all its claim, snatching it up and nailing it to the cross." In Ephesians 2:14, 15, I read, "It is Christ who is our peace, and who made the two of us one by breaking down the barrier of hostility that kept us apart. In his own flesh he abolished the law with its commands and precepts, to create in himself one new man from us who had been two and to make peace."

I felt angry that I had lived by man's standards for perfection. My life had been spent attempting to keep the commandments perfectly but often failing! Jesus was the perfect sin-bearer before God and the *only* atonement for sins.

I felt numb as the impact of the Scriptures sank in. I had never before grasped the meaning of the Bible's truths! My worship was unacceptable before God. Scripture once again confirmed that my acts of penance, reparation, praying the rosary, and participations in religious devotions were totally unacceptable before God. I was convicted anew of my ignorance of God's plan. Why?

A passage I read in Ephesians 2:8 jolted my thinking. I said: "For by *grace* have you been saved through faith; this is *not your own doing,* it is God's gift—not a reward for anything you have accomplished, so let no one pride himself on it."

That was a message of tremendous significance. Throughout my life I was taught and believed that when I was a baby God had sanctified my life with His grace in my spiritual birth at baptism and that grace increased with every worthy reception of one of the sacraments (communion, confession, and confirmation) and with every spiritual meritorious work I performed daily. I was now learning that all my righteousness was as filthy rags before God (Isaiah 64:6). God's Word told me that I could not earn righteousness before Him; that works such as penance and supplication for sins would have no deeper roots than my own strength; and that if I continued to depend on works for security I would ultimately fail and inevitably lose eternal salvation. I was convinced that salvation could not be purchased by any religious or moral actions on my part. Salvation was a gift from God to me, and I was to accept it by faith, in accordance with the simple plan of salvation set forth in the Bible. In pursuit, I had finally learned God's unerring truth in His Word!

As the autumn wind blew rustling leaves about me, my conscience chilled. I had lived on the ragged edge of spiritual destruction, and the compunction to respond to God's gift became overwhelming! Yet, defecting from my father's religion and my heritage frightened me. What would it cost to leave the Roman Catholic faith? I had to choose. I compared what I had known about life and eternity at the beginning of my search to what I now knew. There was no real choice? I had to step out on faith!

During the worship service that morning, my thoughts were exploding. I had trouble focusing on the preacher's message. I wanted to shout to the world my realization of God's love, my sorrow for unrepented sins, and my wish to become "born again."

My decision to put on Christ in baptism had been made during the early-morning walk. In a short time, it seemed that my whole life had passed before me, and I became fully aware that my questions had been answered.

I will never forget the hymn that was sung as I moved slowly up the aisle to meet my Lord in baptism:

There is a fountain filled with blood, drawn from Emmanuel's veins.
And sinners plunged beneath that blood lose all their guilty stains.

Dear dying Lamb, Thy precious blood shall never lose its power . . .
Till all the ransomed church of God be saved to sin no more.

E'er since by faith I saw the stream, Thy flowing wounds supply,
Redeeming love has been my theme, and shall be till I die!

My friend Paul reached out his hands to accept my surrender to God. Hugging me and drawing me close, he whispered, "Welcome home, Joanne." Then, turning me to the assembled congregation, he said, "Most of you know Joanne and the struggles and challenges she has faced in making her life-changing decision. I never fail to stand in awe and wonderment of God's grace. Today, Joanne has come forward to be buried with her Lord in Baptism. Would several of the ladies accompany her to prepare her for this glorious occasion?"

Assisting me with preparation for the baptism was Helen Pearson and Lydia Holby, two of the women who had befriended me during that long and wearisome journey. I thought, "What if someone had not shared with me the simple truth of the Gospel?" The message of redemption was so simple, yet so deeply moving and convicting. Its powerful words had brought me to the fountain of life—Jesus!

Standing in front of the congregation in the baptismal water, clothed in a robe of white, I confessed openly my belief in Jesus, and my desire to be born again. Following the example in I Timothy 6:12, and as the Ethiopian nobleman did in Acts 8:27, I died to my past with Christ and was buried with Him in the water of baptism to arise as a new creature (Romans 6:2-4). After all the public and private presentations I had made in teaching others about religious convictions and consecration, this surrender climaxed my complete dedication to God, to whom I had made a commitment at the tender age of six.

Baptism into Christ (Galatians 3:27) was the transition between my old life and the new in Jesus. Baptism is the only way the Bible teaches that anyone can get "into Christ." Faith had started the salvation process, but the power of the Word of God had changed my thinking and purpose in life. I felt so unworthy, for it was only by God's grace that I was being saved.

Believing in His promises, I was immersed in the water of Baptism. Now justified before my God (Romans 5:9), I had the seal of God's covenant (Acts 2:38, Hebrews 9:15-17, and Hebrews 8:8). Cleansed of all past sins (I John 1:9), I would receive the gift of the Holy Spirit (Acts 2:16-21), and would be admitted into the citizenship of Heaven when I died (Hebrews 10:19).

God had broken my will; through the power of the Gospel I was now a New Testament Christian according to God's plan for salvation.

Amid hugs and smiles of congratulations, and amid my own tears, I recognized that this overwhelming joy and contentment were greater than any cost I could possibly pay. An enormous burden had been lifted from my heart—the load of sin!

I am constantly overwhelmed by the forgiveness I have received because of the sacrifice Jesus made. The law, under which I labored for years, had condemned me in the sight of God, but Jesus redeemed me by His precious blood. I will never have to face the judgment of His almighty righteousness, "for there is therefore now no condemnation [judgment] to them which are in Christ Jesus" (Romans 8:1). My standing before God has been changed from guilt and condemnation to pardon and forgiveness. "Who shall lay anything to the charge of God's elect? It is God that justifieth. Who is he that condemneth? It is Christ that died, yea, rather, that is risen again, who is even at the right hand of God, who also makes intercession for us" (Romans 8:23). Christ had become my wisdom, righteousness, sanctification, and redemption! (I Corinthians 1:30).

I had never known true peace of conscience, mind, and soul until I stood at the foot of the cross and, in obedient faith, identified with Christ's death, burial, and resurrection. Only then did I find the paths of service and peace God had marked out for me.

Philosophies and traditions of men no longer confuse me or influence me, for the Bible's truth is the yardstick by which I measure every false doctrine. I study the scriptures daily, using them for counsel, assurance, hope, and strength to do His will.

I have answered the questions, "Who am I?" "Where am I going?", and "How will I get there?" I have a treasure—the words of eternal life. Ignorance of God held me in bondage until I learned of the redeeming love of Jesus and His desire to free me from mental and spiritual slavery. I John 5:11 states: "And this is the record, that God has given us eternal life and this life is in the Son. He that has the Son has life, and he who does not have the Son of God has not life!"

With clarity I never thought possible, my life now echoes the words of a song written long ago by Fanny J. Crosby:

> Redeemed, how I love to proclaim it! Redeemed by the blood of the Lamb! Redeemed through His infinite mercy, His child and forever I am!
>
> Redeemed and so happy in Jesus; no language my rapture can tell!
> I know that the light of His presence, with me doth continually dwell!
>
> I know I shall see in His beauty, the King in whose law I delight.
> Who lovingly guardeth my footsteps, and giveth me strength in the night.
>
> Redeemed, redeemed! Redeemed by the blood of the Lamb!
> Redeemed—Redeemed! His child and forever I am!

13

Obedience to the Bible —My Life-Changing Habit

My desire for inner peace and truth led me to search the depths of God's Word and discover its immeasurable riches. Through divine revelation, I had asked the most important question of my life: "What does it mean to be saved?" At that point, it did not matter that I belonged to a particular church or that I was basically a good person. Was I saved! Like the believing Jews who questioned their salvation in Acts 2:27, I needed to repent and become immersed in the waters of baptism for the forgiveness of my sins (Acts 2:38).

Confronted with Roman Catholic doctrines that were in complete contradiction to God's inspired teaching, I wrestled with remaining in my parents' religion, or choosing God's plan for salvation. Finally, after many hours of prayer and study of God's promises, I abandoned my life to Jesus and was born again in the waters of baptism.

Today, as a New Testament Christian, I have joy and peace in my heart, knowing that Jesus is my shepherd and will guide and protect me wherever I go. *He* is the joy of my salvation.

I am no longer concerned with man's interpretation of religious commitment. Jesus said in Mark 10:29-31: "I give you my word, there is no one who has given up home, brothers or sisters, mother or father, children or property, for me and for the gospel who will not receive in this present age a hundred times as many homes, brothers and sisters, mothers, children and property—and persecution besides—and in the age to come, everlasting life!" Like Paul, I can truly say, "this one thing I do, thinking not of myself as having reached the finish line. I give no thought to what lies behind but push on to what is ahead. My entire attention is on the finish line as I run toward the prize to which God calls me—life on high in Christ Jesus" (Philippians 3:13, 14).

I now have a "home" with Christian brothers and sisters (my new family). They share with me life's joys and sorrows in the Spirit of the Lord. My brothers and sisters offer me sanctuary in a world where unforeseen circumstances and keen disappointments send the strongest reeling! They inspire and edify me with their commitment as ambassadors for Jesus. It touches me deeply to see one Christian profoundly concerned about another's spiritual welfare. I am proud to be associated with such genuine love for the lost and dying of this world. Each time I assemble with "my family," they remind me of the early Christians, about whom it was said, "See how they love one another!"

Converting from Roman Catholicism to New Testament Christianity required a change from behavioral patterns and attitudes reflecting man's traditions and commandments to ones that were in alignment with God's Word. I have had to acquire a whole new frame of reference in identifying with the church that Jesus founded. For instance, the church in the New Testament was referred to by several names, such as the church of the Lord (Acts 20:28), the church of the firstborn (Hebrews 12:23), and the church of Christ (Romans 16:16).

The Roman Catholic hierarchial power ties each parish and diocese together in a chain of command. The Book of Acts emphasizes the importance of and endorses the autonomy of the local church—the church that Jesus founded. Christ's church has no headquarters on earth. No congregation has any authority over another. Christ is the only head of His church, and of each congregation. In Him alone is invested supreme authority (Matthew 28:18) as the only high priest (Hebrews 5:5, 6) and the only mediator between God and mankind (I Timothy 2:5). He had been given authority and power to reconcile mankind with God (Acts 4:12) and to petition for blessings for "those who draw near to God through Him" (Hebrews 7:25). Jesus is the only priest who scripturally serves as an intermediary between God and man. He, alone, for all time ministered with His own blood to make an efficacious atonement for the sins of mankind.

Each congregation of the Lord's church has its own elders to oversee the flock as suggested in Acts 14:23, but not to dominate over those in their charge (I Peter 5:3). "Elders" are also called "bishops" (Titus 1:5,7), "pastors" (Ephesians 4:11), or the "presbytery" (I Timothy 4:14). Qualifications for elders (or bishops, pastors, or the presbytery) are clearly outlined in I Timothy 3, Titus 1, I Peter 5 and Acts 20. My responsibility to the elders is to esteem them highly in love (I Thessalonians 5:12,13) and to be subject to them (Hebrews 13:17).

Deacons, likewise, are appointed by each congregation, according to qualifications set forth in I Timothy 3:8-12 and Acts 6:3. There is no authority for one elder, or one bishop, to have authority over other elders or bishops, nor for one congregation to have authority over another congregation.

The preacher is the evangelist or minister of the Word of God. The Greek word for preacher, "Kerus," means "a herald of the king." The preacher is to evangelize or win souls for God, as all followers are commanded to do. He is to edify the local church (Ephesians 4:11-16), defend the faith (I Timothy 1:3; Galatians 1:8-9; Jude verse 3) and train preachers and teachers (I Timothy 2:2). A preacher is not a pastor, as many have been led to believe, unless he also serves as an elder.

The church that Jesus instituted has no written creed or dogmas of faith other than the Bible itself! II John 1:9 states specifically: "Anyone who goes ahead and does not abide in the doctrine of Christ does not have God, he who abides in the doctrine has both the Father and the Son." In Galatians 1:8,9 the apostle said: "For even if we, or an angel from heaven, should preach to you a gospel not in accord with the one we delivered to you, let a curse be upon him! I repeat what I have just said: if anyone preaches a gospel to you other than the one you received, let a curse be upon him!" According to the Bible, groups that depart from the Scripture's authority have refused to recognize the church that Christ Himself established.

The Bible gives no example of anyone being voted into the church, but offers salvation to all. The Bible teaches that one must be a member of the Lord's church (the church of the New Testament) to be saved, for it is by one Spirit that we are all baptized into one body (II Corinthians 12:13) and then added to the church by the Lord (Acts 2:47).

The most difficult concept I encountered was this: in the eyes of God, I am a priest! As a Roman Catholic, I accepted the priest as God's divinely appointed authority figure on earth. Until I understood the concept of the Mosaic Law (or the Old Covenant), I was not aware that the Roman Catholic Church had incorporated many Old Covenant teachings into its religious doctrines, including that of priests. Under the Old Covenant, a believer rested his faith in only symbols and types of Christ, and the Law was placed before the believer for compliance. However, under the New Covenant, the believer puts his trust in the actual person of the Lord Jesus Himself and in His deed of atonement. Jesus Himself said that He came to *fulfill* the Old Covenant and to institute the new covenant, which He did through His death, burial, and resurrection.

Long before leaving Roman Catholicism, I had questioned the priest's authority to petition God on my behalf. How often I had seen extremely inadequate spiritual leaders (saying one thing and doing another) attempt to intercede on my behalf. In the New Testament, the church of Christ (of which I am now a member) is a priesthood, and every believer is a priest (I Peter 2:5, 9; Revelation 1:6; 5:10) who offers sacrifices of praise and sharing (I Peter 2:5; Hebrews 13:15, 16), monetary giving (Philippians 4:18), and humility (Romans 12:1, 2). I am profoundly honored to belong to God's royal priesthood! I now deal with Him directly through "the" great high priest—Jesus Christ, Himself!

As a Roman Catholic, I was taught "that a saint is someone who has lived his or her life on earth in an exemplary manner, not only observing the laws of God and the Church, but attaining a high degree of heroic holiness." I was encouraged to seek the intercession of Mary ("the blessed mother") and the saints.

The Council of Trent decreed, and I believed, that the saints who reign together with Christ offer up their own prayers to God for me. As a Roman Catholic I was taught it was good and useful to invoke the saints and have recourse to them for obtaining benefits from God. The Scriptures teach nothing about the living being blessed by prayers to or through the dead. Only through Jesus Christ may our prayers be heard (II Timothy 2:5). In fact, the Bible uses the word "saint" to refer to all Christians—living people, not just those who have died. Paul addressed the churches at Ephesus, Philippi, Corinth, and those at Rome as "saints." Also the Bible repeatedly condemns attempts to commune with the dead (Isaiah 8:19, 20).

As a Roman Catholic, I was taught that devotion to Mary was the way to Christ. She was my intercessor, my hope, my message-bearer before the throne of God. As a child, crowning Mary as the Queen of Heaven and earth was a special event, and it was a privilege for any girl to crown Mary as the "May Queen!" My relationship to Mary as the "Mother of God" was very tender, loving, affectionate, and devoted. I sincerely believed she loved me as my own mother did, and would do everything within her power as God's mother to protect and guide me through this vale of tears.

Since childhood, I had believed that praying the "Hail Mary" would present my petitions before God: "Hail Mary, full of grace, the Lord is with Thee. Blessed art thou among women and blessed is the fruit of thy womb, Jesus. Holy Mary, Mother of God, pray for us sinners, now and at the hour of our death. Amen." But, in Matthew 6:7-13, Jesus tells us that repetitious prayer is not pleasing to God. "In your prayer do not rattle on like the pagans. They think they will win a hearing by the sheer multiplication of words. Do not imitate them, for your father in Heaven knows what you need before you ask him." Just as you would not want someone saying the same thing over and over again to you, God wants our prayers to be the words of the heart and not a memorized prayer whose words quickly lose their meaning if repeated over and over again.

Nowhere did the Bible proclaim Mary superior to other human beings. The Scripture used to exalt Mary above all other women (Luke 1:28: "Blessed art thou among women") merely pronounces her blessed, not divine. In Judges 5:24, a similar blessing was pronounced upon Jael: "Blessed above women shall Jael, the wife of Heber, the Kenite, be." Likewise, I learned that even the doctrine of Mary's assumption into Heaven is contradictory! In John 3:13, we are told, "No man hath ascended up to Heaven, but He that came down from Heaven, even the

Son of Man which is in Heaven—Jesus Christ, Himself." At God's right hand He is our only mediator. He is the one who blesses us, not His mother. Jesus alone is the Way, the Truth, and the Light! No Scripture instructs me to glorify Mary and pray to her. To do so would desecrate Christ's position as the only mediator and intercessor before the Father in Heaven. My admiration for Mary as the mother of Jesus remains untouched. Truly she is blessed, because she was chosen to carry God's Son.

Years ago, I truly believed I had been chosen by Christ to be "set apart," to be His Bride. My whole life was meant for surrender and serving. Unhindered by materialism, I lived a life of poverty, chastity, and obedience.

Born from above, again, I am wed to Christ as a member of His church, which is His bride. As a "sister" in the family of God, I testify to the marvels of God's free and abundant grace. I am now a saint, a person "set apart" from the world to testify of God's grace and to herald salvation's message wherever I go.

As a nun, I learned well the art of discipline. Today, I use that discipline to meditate on and study God's precious Word. Each day for a period of a half hour or more I prepare for the work God will give me leading other souls through my example and words of encouragement.

Stewardship comes easily because of the vow of poverty. When a nun, I had no worldly wealth, so all I now have is on loan from God. He has promised to fulfill my needs, (Matthew 6:25-34), and has blessed me with material blessings.

The vow of chastity taught me the principles of love, and the realization that God is "a jealous God" (Exodus 20:5), Savior of my soul and Lord of my life. As His bondservant, it is "no longer I who live, but Christ who lives in me!" (Galatians 2:20). God is designing my life, as a potter molds his clay and refines it into beauty and excellence.

I love to share God's Word with "my people" (my former family), Roman Catholics. As a nun, I did not evangelize or share truth, or even know that I should! I now want to spend and be spent, giving everything I have to reflect God's glory and manifold grace.

The obligation of following God as the author of truth is imperative in our lives! The truth cost Jesus His very life. You and I must be willing to pay whatever price is necessary in our search for truth, and when we find it we must be willing to embrace it! John tells us (chapter 8, verse 32), "you shall know the truth and the truth will make you free."

If you are seeking a deeper faith, renewed trust, and selfless love, I invite you to investigate this testimony. Do you know Christ? Are you sure you are saved? Perhaps you've been thinking, "I want to be *sure* I am ready for death. I want my sins forgiven and my guilt removed. I want to be with Jesus eternally."

As a loving Father, God longs to forgive us if we will only acknowledge sin, forsake pride and selfishness, and follow His plan for forgiveness. He wants to remove any hindrances to our communication.

I believe we can never experience complete emotional healing or fully receive God's love unless we understand God's sorrow over our sin and selfishness. The Bible teaches that there is a difference between godly sorrow and worldly sorrow. Paul wrote to the Corinthian Christians: "I rejoice, not because you were grieved, but because you were grieved into repenting, for you felt a godly grief, so that you suffered no loss through us. For godly grief produces a repentance that leads to salvation and brings no regret, but worldly grief produces death" (II Corinthians 7:10).

Godly sorrow requires more than confession. If we confess sins, but keep practicing them, we have not really experienced godly grief. Repentance is not simply "feeling bad" about what we have done. Sometimes we feel bad if we get caught, or if we have to stop sinning. Godly sorrow does not depend on feelings or selfish motives. It is concerned with *how sin hurts God and other people!* True repentance produces a change in our habits and a new respect for God's laws. Unless we are willing to take our stubborn wills and put them under God's control, we have not given our total allegiance to Him.

God has not only grieved over our sins; He has done something about them. He has given His own Son as a sacrifice. You and I deserved to be punished, but God sent Jesus to take our punishment.

Salvation can be yours, dear soul. He offers His gift of love freely to you and yearns for you to put Him at the center of your life. The only return He asks is for you to surrender your will and renounce all values, beliefs, and actions that have condemned you before Him. Think! If you choose God's salvation plan, you will one day be stepping on the shores of eternity and finding it Heaven! You will be touching a hand and finding it God's hand. You will be breathing a new air and finding it celestial air! You will feel invigorated and discover you are immortal! As you pass from the tempest of this earthly life to the unknown calm of eternity, you will discover that, at last, you are home with God!

This is God's simple plan for salvation, documented with Scriptural references in this book:

    (1) Believe that Jesus is the Christ, the Son of God.

    (2) Repent of your past sinful life.

    (3) Confess your faith publicly.

    (4) Be baptized into Christ for forgiveness; "wash away your sins in the blood of Christ," as the apostle Paul was told to do (Acts 22:15).

    (5) Allow Jesus' example and teachings to guide your life.

We live in troubled times—days of uncertainty, religious divisions, confusing philosophies, doctrinal error, and threat of nuclear annihilation. Jesus came to this earth so that you and I might have life and have it more abundantly. He died a horrible death to save us from a wasted life! He wants you to let Him into your heart and your life. He wants to fill the emptiness that has existed there for such a long time. God waits patiently for you to "come home," whatever your past, your problems, or your present needs. Jesus is the only one to whom you can turn to fill the voids that exist in your life. He is the only one who fully understands your pain, your trials and your heartaches. In Isaiah 30:18, we are told: "The Lord waits to be gracious to you!" Romans 2:4 asks: "Do you not know that God's kindness is meant to lead you to repentance?"

God waits with outstretched arms: "Come unto me, and I will give you rest!" The happiness you will receive in this life is more than you could ever dream of, and eternity will be the climax of your dreams!

Are you saved, based on what you have read and learned from God's word, or are you depending on the doctrines of man? Is your faith in God strong enough that you will follow Him and trust in Him alone? The answer you give could mean life—or death!—in eternity! May God be with you, dear friend, as you walk His pathways. I pray that we will meet one day at the throne of God—to sing His praises forever. This is the very reason we were created!

Epilogue

In the Book of Ecclesiastes (3:1-3), the writer describes the seasons of life, explaining that in each one's life there is a time for every matter under heaven. Throughout the chapter, he alludes to the uselessness of human striving which is not lived in fellowship with God and in accord with His divine will. Summarizing the duty of man, he says, "Fear God and keep His commandments."

Since my conversion to the Gospel, my life has been a time of emotional and spiritual growth amidst the predictable crises and unexpected crossroads of human experiences. The most striking difference has been my ability to remain unshaken and committed to my new identity as a Christian. An inner gulf of confusion and deception has been crossed, and I now have a new degree of inner strength and equilibrium. I attribute this change to God's grace working in my life and the guidance of the Holy Spirit, which I implore daily.

Perhaps the most notable growth has been the diligent study and pursuit I have given to the study of God's Word. In Romans 8:19-32 I read that the Gospel is the power of God for salvation—present and future. Since I discovered God's Word as a source of deep inner emotional peace and strength, I have committed my life to sharing its message to those who are in desperate need of help and guidance. God's Word tells me to always be ready to give an answer for the hope that lies within. As a counselor and teacher, my prayer is that I can communicate God's word of life to those who are helpless and hopeless, adrift on the sea of life, with no place to cast their anchor. It is my desire that my life will be used as one of Christ's agents of healing in their broken world of sin and suffering.

In searching desperately for answers to the questions "Who am I? Where am I going? and How will I get there?" I have found a treasure I never dreamed available—the words of eternal life through the Bible. I have found the "real" Jesus, who cared enough for me to remove me from the mental and spiritual slavery that had bound me to fears of guilt, doubt, and self-destruction. As a former Roman Catholic, God prepared me for the master plan of my life and groomed me in my youth and young adult life for the great commission I have today.

Just as the apostle Paul was a man of bold resolve as he sought to convey the gospel message to all who would listen, so too am I committed in standing firm in telling the story of God's mercy and love "in season and out of season" (II Timothy 4:11).

The tape of my life is now rewound spiritually. Although very fine instruments may be able to pick up recordings of my actions and thinking that are, and perhaps will always be, a part of my Roman Catholic heritage, I pray daily that the blood of Jesus and my growth in the knowledge and wisdom of God's Word will shine through my life and be the beckoning call that will lead others to Christ and strengthen those in the brotherhood. To God be the glory!

Printed in the United States
35379LVS00006B/382-396